Mikwaiti

"My Hope"

~ ~ A Horsewoman's Journey with God ~ ~

To Robert +
Danielle
May your dreams
come true!
Love,
Pat
(1 Cor. 10:31)

Pat Rotisky

TRILOGY
PROFESSIONAL PUBLISHING MEETS POWERFUL PROMOTION

A wholly owned subsidiary of TBN

Mikwaiti, "My Hope"

Trilogy Christian Publishers A Wholly Owned Subsidiary of Trinity Broadcasting Network

2442 Michelle Drive Tustin, CA 92780

Rights Department, 2442 Michelle Drive, Tustin, CA 92780.

Trilogy Christian Publishing/TBN and colophon are trademarks of Trinity Broadcasting Network.

For information about special discounts for bulk purchases, please contact Trilogy Christian Publishing.

Trilogy Disclaimer: The views and content expressed in this book are those of the author and may not necessarily reflect the views and doctrine of Trilogy Christian Publishing or the Trinity Broadcasting Network.

Manufactured in the United States of America

10 9 8 7 6 5 4 3 2 1

Library of Congress Cataloging-in-Publication Data is available.

ISBN: 978-1-63769-610-1

E-ISBN: 978-1-63769-611-8

Dedication

To all of my equine partners—

who have taught me far more

than I could have ever imagined possible.

Acknowledgments

Several key people have assisted and encouraged me in this project to whom thanks are due, namely: my husband, Frank Rotisky, for his personal input and generous support of not only this manuscript but of each equestrian escapade in which he enthusiastically cheered me on.

I also owe a debt of gratitude to Jane Saxton-Hoch, who has voluntarily and enthusiastically read through, retyped, and copyedited these memoirs, encouraging me to see this project through to the end, trusting that God has a special use for it in-store. I have appreciated her insight as I trust Him for sending her into my life at this particular time. Jane also recruited her daughter, Meghan Hoch, as another set of professionally trained eyes to oversee this manuscript. To round out the family involvement, husband and father, Dan Hoch, used his expertise and equipment to scan, in the necessary 300dpi, the various and sundry pictures

I desired to include with the narrative—which was of immense relief to me.

Additional thanks are due to another dear friend, Alicia Anderson, for her skillful editing advice and earnest encouragement in pursuing this publication.

I am privileged to have had such loving and loyal partners who not only gave their time and talent on my behalf but also their very valuable input all the way to the final jot and title.

A Special Thanks

The following stories of day-to-day events with various horses give evidence of God's sovereign attention to the desires of the heart that are directed toward Him in an effort to "seek first" His kingdom and righteousness. Indeed, He added "all these things" (Matthew 6:33), often using people who were completely unaware that they were God's tools of blessing to me.

One individual in particular, Barbara Parkening, deserves my deepest thanks for her many kindnesses and her generous spirit, not only to me but also to so many others. It is a debt I could never repay since my equestrian escapades might never have happened if it were not for her. To this day, more than two dozen years and a half-dozen horses later, she remains one of my most treasured friends.

Table of Contents

Table of Contents

Preface

This journal is wonderfully written by a godly woman who shares her hopes and hurts—and honors God by doing so. You do not have to have a horse to be blessed by this very fine, easy read, and strongly encouraging love story.

Pat writes regarding the book's purpose: "In this book, I have set out to kill two birds with one stone: I provide a look into the horseshow world through my relationships, both human and equine, and I demonstrate how each experience pointed to Christ through my growing faith. These chapters feature recurring themes involving God's dealings with my understanding of what He was teaching me, not only about Himself but also about His purposes for others with whom I had come into contact. The repetition of these ideas, in different contexts and settings, further shows God's consistency and faithfulness."

Pat more than accomplishes her task, and she does so with an easy-to-read style, stocked with many pictures and stories—a few sad ones too. Let's put it this way; she did not dodge the hard stuff. Pat rarely does—and this is difficult to do for some authors—to tell of the hurt, freely writing of both the joys and deep sorrows. Anyone in grief over the loss of a beloved animal will be able to relate to Pat's enthusiastic journey mingled with heartfelt hurt.

The Lord Jesus who created us, if you are saved, is currently building a place in the New Jerusalem—in the New Earth. The first one had animals and was called very good by the Lord at its conclusion. I can foresee God who made the original animals, using His DNA, to make animals familiar to us be a part of the end-time blessing, and it will again be very good.

You will find this is truly a heart-swelling book more than a horse book alone—both themes are so beautifully intertwined so as not to be able to determine at times which is the dominant characteristic—which is the way it should be: the love for the horse, and/or the horse's love for Pat, culminating in the final analysis of God's intense love for both.

I trust you will enjoy Pat Rotisky's *Mikwaiti, "My Hope"—A Horsewoman's Journey with God* © 2021.

—Gregory H. Harris, ThD

Emeritus Professor of Bible Exposition,

The Master's Seminary—

Introduction

According to the ancient wisdom literature of the Bible, King Solomon said, *"The writing of many books is endless, and excessive devotion to books is wearying to the body"* (Ecclesiastes 12:12). So, it is with some fear and trepidation that I pursue this course, lest it is just another addition to the stack. Nevertheless, I have written my thirty-five years of equine memoirs as a Christian testimony that hopefully will encourage you whether you are a horseperson or not.

This book has been a labor of love. In a sense, it completes a project I began many years ago as I found an astounding connection between my horseback riding and my faith. But I tucked the narrative away for various reasons, because I just was not ready to make it a full-blown project and assumed no one else would be interested. My abandonment of the task, however, was not without my learning an enormous amount about horses, riding, and especially putting feet (or hoofs, if you'll pardon the pun) to my faith along the way.

Encouragement from my friend, Jane Saxton, inspired me to unearth my writings and resume the project, especially since she was willing to edit it for me. I found that remembering, writing, and pursuing the finished product to be a very satisfying experience.

In this book, I have set out to kill two birds with one

stone: I provide a look into the horseshow world through my relationships, both human and equine, and I demonstrate how each experience pointed to Christ through my growing faith. These chapters feature recurring themes involving God's dealings with my understanding of what He was teaching me, not only about Himself but also about His purposes for others with whom I had come into contact. The repetition of these ideas in different contexts and settings further shows God's consistency and faithfulness.

Neither a horse expert nor a Bible scholar, I profoundly appreciate those who are. I hope that in these pages, my enthusiasm for horses and for God is apparent and even contagious. As God speaks to us through our everyday pursuits, how can we forego the privilege and opportunity He gives us to gaze into His character, purposes, love, and redemptive plan for our lives?

All the Pretty Horses

My story begins early, in stops, and starts. I have always admired horses and had faintly thought about them from a young age, but being a city girl from Detroit, I never considered being around them much of a possibility. My only recollection of horses while growing up on the east side was at Belle Isle Park, a US island in the middle of the Detroit River between the shores of downtown Detroit and Windsor, Ontario. That was our park—our playground. It was a long walk, but my three older sisters and I managed to make the trek across the half-mile bridge to get to our favorite beach in the summer.

On the island, there was a vendor who had a string of ponies hooked to a motorized gizmo that made them walk in a circle. They were probably overworked and under-groomed, but to me, they were beautiful creatures. I recall once, when I was very young, being strapped into a big western saddle and moving around the circle on this wonderful thing called a horse, my small body being forced to sway back and forth with the movement of the rotund belly. My little head bobbed up and down like one of those bobblehead dolls we used to see in the back windows of cars.

Once I got older, I was allowed to take a horseback ride through the Belle Isle woods. It was not very dense, and since the island was only five miles in circumference, there was no danger of getting lost. But once inside the woods, I forgot where I was as my imagination took over. I enjoyed the thrill of being on the horse's back, even if the ride was just nose-to-tail, single-file, and led by a guide. The group was only allowed to walk the horses, never to trot or canter.

My father, Dan Beattie, inadvertently fostered my fascination with the equine species. Before I was born, he wrote for his own radio program in Washington, DC, called *Government Girl*—the heroine having been created after his sweetheart, Helen Smith, who was a secretary to a US senator at the time. They married, and years later, his young family moved to Detroit, where I was born. He furthered his writing career as a scriptwriter for *The Green Hornet, Sergeant Preston of the Yukon (and his dog, King!)*, and the very popular, *The Lone Ranger*, which aired on WXYZ Radio. We four girls grew up watching the Lone Ranger ride a beautiful white stallion named Silver, with his Indian sidekick, Tonto, galloping alongside on a pinto pony called Scout.

My sister, Gloria ("Glo"), and I were citified cowgirls—tomboys at heart. Since she was older than I was, she always got to be the Lone Ranger in our "let's pretend" games, while I got to be Tonto. I loved everything about him, especially his spotted pony, which perhaps was a peek into my future. If there was some other TV western that we liked, she played the lead, and I was always the sidekick. That was okay, though, because she had to think up the storyline, and all I had to do was play along and have fun getting rescued from some make-believe villain. Carol and Peggy, the two eldest, could have cared less, being interested in more feminine pursuits. Nevertheless, each Christmas, Glo and I hoped to find cowboy boots, double-holsters, and cap guns under the tree instead of dolls.

When the neighborhood vendor brought his Shetland pony around offering rides for a dollar, our game became more real. Glo was big enough to have her picture taken sitting atop a pinto pony just like Tonto's, all dressed up in the western regalia of chaps, vest, bandana, pistols, and a sombrero. Regrettably, I was too little, but that was the greatest fun I could have imagined.

Finding Faith

When I moved away from home as a young adult to Los Angeles, I began the life of surviving on my own. Not only did I put horses out of my mind, but I also forewent practicing any religious upbringing I had. Ingrained in me since a small child was my mother's faithful pursuit of church on Sundays and parochial school for the four of us girls through each of our twelve years.

It was easy to let all of that go as an eighteen-year-old now totally on her own, particularly one enamored by the Hollywood lifestyle and the warm California climate. The next few years followed the twists and turns of meeting people, making friends, dating, and finally getting married at twenty-two years old. The ceremony had been back in Detroit, a formal church wedding with my entire family in attendance. I was so excited to wear my mother's beautiful French-silk wedding dress with the long train following me down the aisle of the church where we had grown up.

But a failing marriage at the age of twenty-four compelled me to go home again—this time in desperation to be with my family. Once I got there, the first thing I asked of my mother was to take me to church. After all, we had been taught that divorce was not supposed to be an option. Now it all came crashing down around me. So, we stopped there on our way home from the airport. Through tears, I confessed every big and little sin to the priest after years of absence, and he comfortingly said to me, "God is pleased that you have returned to Him." Although I had expected him to "throw the book" at me, the penance he gave me was surprisingly light. As I prayed privately, I said the few prayers I had been assigned and then cried out in my heart to God, "Lord, I have made such a mess of my life—please take it over!" I did not know exactly what that would mean or what I was saying at the time, but my simple plea was the beginning of a series of amazing events that would lead me to the truths of the Bible, where in years to come, I would find comfort, life's answers, and a determination to help others discover a personal path to the living God through Jesus Christ.

After the long flight and being in a state of deep sorrow and depression, all I wanted to do was sleep. Mom put me into her big bed upstairs, and my tired body succumbed to the depth of darkness that overwhelmed my mind. I don't know how long I slept, but I began to be awakened by the most ethereal, beautiful, indescribable sounds, almost like music but not, almost like singing but not. My mind was full of the beauty of light as the sound filled every corner. It seemed to last only a few seconds or a nano-second at the least, but it was eternally uplifting my soul. As I stirred and began to reluctantly awaken to my world, the darkness of depression quickly closed in, and the mysterious beauty was gone. It wasn't until much later, as I studied the Bible, that the Lord revealed to my heart the verse that "There is joy in the presence of the angels of God over one sinner who repents" (Luke 15:10). That was what I had experienced on that first day of desperately submitting to God in turning from my sin, and the thought of it still fills my heart with great wonder!

However, my relationship with God took time for me to understand. I hadn't yet learned any scriptural truth, much less how to pray, other than, "Help, God!" So, my encounter described above had not yet produced in me any spiritual growth or understanding—it was definitely not an overnight transformation. I had to be broken before I could be blessed. I struggled for the next month in Detroit, unable to eat, losing weight, still overtaken by depression, and on the brink of suicide (but too afraid to commit it). I began to beg God in my heart, telling Him I would do anything He wanted if He would just save my marriage. At least now I believed He heard me.

My mother invited me to a prayer meeting that her local church was conducting where personal prayers were made to the Holy Spirit, luring me with the promise that they would pray for my marriage. That was all I needed to hear; however, upon arrival, I was so very devastated emotionally that all I could do was sit with my head lowered and listen. People started talking about answers to specific prayers they had received, and *that* was new to me! In all my years of religious training, all I had ever known were memorized prayers, albeit many of them beautifully written, but none of them personal to me or specific to my given need. The reality of God being intimately involved in my life was far removed from my heart and experience. Yet, an example of living faith was shown to me by my mother during that month I was home with her. She had not just belonged to a religion, but in time I realized she had given her heart to her Savior—not to a religion or specific denomination.

Her influence on my young life as a child brings the memory of my cutting out what I called "Holy Pictures" from her many religious magazines, and pasting them into a scrapbook, while my other little girlfriends were playing with cut-out dolls. Also, one evening when I was about nine, we were in the basement while mother was ironing. I was sitting on the floor watching a religious movie like *The Greatest Story Ever Told*. It came to the final scene where Jesus met His disciples in the upper room after His resurrection. "Doubting Thomas" had just articulated his doubt—and Jesus challenged him to put his fingers into the nail holes in his hands, and his hand into His side saying, "Do not be unbelieving, but believing" at which time, Thomas exclaimed, *"My Lord and my God!"* (John 20:26-28). Then the actor playing Jesus turned his body to the camera, looked straight out of the TV box, his eyes catching the wide-eyed gaze of a nine-year-old sitting cross-legged on the floor, and He said, *"Because you have seen*

Me, have you believed? Blessed are they who did not see, and yet believed" (verse 29). I was moved with excitement. I swung around to face my mother, exclaiming, "Mommy, Mommy! We haven't seen Jesus, but we believe, right, Mommy? So, we are blessed?!'" "That's right, honey," she said reassuringly. Another small seed of faith was planted in my heart that day, and I still thank God for her example of faith and faithfulness to me these many years later.

Back at the prayer meeting, my mother told the group why I had come. Everyone gathered around and laid their hands on me, praying that God would save my marriage. That gave me a little bit of hope amidst the depression under which I was buried. After about a month and a few prayer meetings later, I sensed it was time for me to go back to my home in California to see what I could salvage of my life. I was terrified but felt at least I had a new purpose. *Maybe the Lord had me come here just to find these prayer meetings so that I can look for the same thing in Los Angeles,* I thought. My mother agreed and encouraged me, and I was instilled with enough fortitude to return to our empty Burbank apartment because I knew that my husband had moved all of his belongings out while I was gone. In my loneliness, I clung to thoughts of the Lord. For some strange reason, however, as soon as I opened the front door, with no aforethought or hint from anyone, I walked straight over to the coat closet, grabbed the Ouija board (all fun and games I had once thought) off the top shelf, marched right back down the stairs and threw it into the giant black garbage dumpster. God was already directing my steps to protect my spiritual walk with Him!

Without further hesitation though, I began my bargaining with God. *If I go to mass and communion seven days a week, then will you save my marriage?* Since I worked as a secretary at Blue Cross in Hollywood, I decided to attend Blessed Sacrament Church on Hollywood Boulevard during my lunch hour. My first mass on Monday was typical; I received communion but felt terribly alone. No one made eye contact, no one spoke. When mass was over, I stayed a while after people left and uttered another one of my very new personal prayers to God: *Lord, why am I here? How can I find one of those prayer meetings?!* I was very discouraged and was about to give up—thinking that perhaps I had completely misunderstood: maybe God didn't really care about my personal problems. Maybe He didn't hear my personal prayers after all.

I made my way to the vestibule, looked around at pamphlets that were meaningless to me, and dejectedly headed for the door. There was only one person left around, a gentleman, Tony, who opened the door for me as I started to exit. Brushing past him, he said gently, "Would you be interested in attending a prayer meeting on Tuesday night?" I nearly jumped up and down in total shock. *"Yes!"* I exclaimed! *How could this be? Is this a coincidence!?* I wondered. He gave me his address, the time to meet, and said he would drive. I *never* considered that I was going to meet a strange man, alone, near his home in Hollywood of all places, and get into his car! My need blinded me to the potential danger; however, it was not a coincidence that placed Tony there at that time; it was a God-incidence!

As we drove, I told him of my shock at his invitation and said that it was *almost* like an answer to prayer. He confidently said it *was* an answer to prayer, no doubt about it! That was the first answer to my personal prayer I had ever prayed and received. I was stunned. Then I began to explain to Tony my failed marriage and my desperation to save it. Once we arrived, his little group of a half-dozen believers prayed over me for God to "save my marriage." I found new encouragement and hope. After that time, Toni eventually introduced me to other young women from the church, and the five of us began a prayer meeting in the basement of Blessed Sacrament Church that worshipped and glorified God each week, with Tony as our leader. I had never experienced such joy in the Lord and fellowship with other believers before, despite my unchanging circumstances.

Months went by, and various attempts at reconciliation with my husband proved fruitless. I managed to get him to a prayer meeting with me, but he was not interested in pursuing the Lord in a personal way. Indeed, he had been unfaithful and broken our marriage covenant with other women with no desire to repent and truly reconcile. So, I was soon grateful that the Lord had *not* answered my prayer as I had prayed it—but indeed had been protecting me from an insincere, convoluted relationship that would have continued to bring me nothing but confusion and grief. God's answer to my prayer was, "No, I will not save your marriage, but I will save you eternally and set you on a better plan for your life with Me."

Jesus had become my husband as I learned more and more of the Scriptures and grew in His grace and love. Finally, I began to meet new Christian friends at work, including one nice fellow who was also broken-hearted over having recently lost his wife and very young son. Our common pain brought us together while we met over coffee breaks. His name was Frank, and he gently began to disciple me with truths from the Bible. He soon could tell that I loved the Lord with all my heart. But one day, he asked me, "Patti, are you saved?" My answer was definite (although unfamiliar with that term): "Yes! I don't have any horrible sins on my soul!" Which, to me, meant that if I died right then and there, at least I would not go to hell at that moment. Frank clarified the beautiful simplicity of the Scriptural truth about trusting in Jesus for our salvation and assurance of heaven. Ephesians 2:8-9 says, *"For by grace you are saved through faith, and that not of yourselves, it is the gift of God; not as a result of works, so that no one may boast."* In other words, no sin I could ever commit could, from now on, separate me from the love of Christ Jesus.

It was not long before Frank invited me to join his group in a Bible study that was being held at UCLA con-ducted by Hal Lindsey. That was where I heard my first message about salvation by grace as a gift and not something I had to do to keep myself saved from the fires of hell. Pastor Lindsey expounded on Romans 8:1, which says, *"Therefore there is now no condemnation for those who are in Christ Jesus."* Through faith in Christ, we are no longer condemned by God. The sinless Jesus who died on the cross for our sins set us free from the bondage of sin and death hanging over our lives. What a relief I felt that night! I was filled with the real, deep-seated joy of my salvation for the first time. I was forgiven; my soul was a clean slate—forever, because of what Jesus did for me personally! Frank later bought me my first study Bible loaded with footnotes and teaching tools which I treasure to this day.

In compensation for the emotional suffering I had endured through my separation and ultimate divorce, it seemed to me, the Lord took away "Elmer Fudd" and brought "Prince Charming" into my life when I finally married Frank about two years later. Together we found a solid Bible-teaching church where we were privileged to learn the Word of God verse by verse for forty years.

My prayer is that, throughout this book, you will find answers to the various dilemmas that confront you no matter what your occupation, vocation, or trivial pursuit. There are always lessons—and there are always answers. Keep reading, and perhaps you will see what I mean.

CHAPTER 1

"Remember the Horse!"

"I will remember the works of the Lord:
Surely I will remember Your wonders of old.
I will also meditate on all Your work,
and talk of Your deeds."
(Psalm 77:11-12, NKJV)

More than twenty years after my move to California and shortly after my fortieth birthday, it was just another routine day on my way to work in a full-time position at our church located in the Valley north of Los Angeles. I loved working there and considered myself as being in full-time ministry. Driving down a Los Angeles freeway, I saw a sign: "Riding lessons, call—." Suddenly my childhood memories revived the attraction to ride that I had buried deep inside. I said to myself, *If I don't do it now, I never will! Go for it!* Having been married by this time to Frank for ten years but with no children of our own, I felt the freedom to call and book my first riding lesson for the following Saturday morning. This reignited what became my lifelong love affair with horses.

I made a commitment with the instructor to train on an equine "schoolmaster" once a week, beginning with how to put on a saddle and bridle. Periodically, my husband, Frank, would stop by to watch me practice. I was what we called a "late bloomer;" other students in my group sessions ranged from the very young (seven or eight years old) through the teenage years. Most riders my age had been at it for many years, if not most of their lives. I would watch the others ride confidently while I struggled—not only to find my balance but trying not to foster a twinge of envy and regret that I hadn't started earlier. I didn't let those thoughts daunt my spirits, however. My opportunity had come, and I was determined to do well.

I soon realized that riding once a week was hardly enough practice to really learn anything. I was at a barn that specialized in training riders to jump their mounts over various-sized fences, and I was looking forward to getting to the point where I could control the horse over my first fence. But at each week's lesson, I had to relearn what I had just learned the previous week, and I knew that confidence and balance were going to come very slowly at that pace. I decided I needed to take lessons twice a week, which would at least provide more practice and give me an opportunity to advance. After about three months, I finally did jump my first small fence. It was exhilarating! I was riding a horse named Rocket, who was trained as a jumper, and I was beginning to feel a little more confident in the saddle.

Not Child's Play

One evening our instructor was going to train us to jump over two fences in a row, so our class of about six riders was full of smiles and anticipation. I was chosen to go first. I put Rocket into a trot, and we headed for the first fence—I was in a two-point position, standing on the balls of my feet in the stirrups, balancing my body in a crouched position over his withers, the highest point of his back. I extended my arms to give his neck and head freedom to stretch, and he cleared the low fence easily. However, the momentum of jumping caused him to pick up the canter as he landed on the other side of the fence. That was fine—his pace was slow, he was under control, and we were headed straight for the second fence. *At this pace*, I thought, *it should be a breeze*—but it wasn't. For some reason, I expected him to take the fence without a hitch, but it seems he expected me to *make* him take it. He got to the fence, planted his front left foot, and made a hard-right turn! He didn't go over the fence, but I did! Flying through the air was certainly a new sensation, but landing on the ground with a hard thud wasn't as enjoyable! Having the wind knocked out of me, I couldn't move right away and just laid there in a pile, moaning. I couldn't tell if I was badly hurt since I seemed to hurt everywhere. It took a minute or two for my brain to sort out everything my abused body was feeling. Finally, I managed to get off my left arm and roll myself over. But I couldn't move my left leg—a strange feeling actually, when the brain tells the body to do something, and it doesn't do it. People came to help me up, and I realized I couldn't walk. "Something is really wrong," I told Frank when I spoke to him with a quivering voice over the phone.

After Frank came to pick me up, we went to the emergency room and learned that I had broken one of my pelvic bones. If two bones on the same side had been broken, I would have been hospitalized in traction. But since that wasn't the case, the doctor sent me home with crutches and told me to lay still and stay home from work for two weeks. There was nothing they could do—no way to put a cast on it—it just had to heal on its own, and that would take about two months. The worst part of it was that I couldn't ride during that time!

When I woke up the next morning, I felt no pain at all if I just sat still on the side of the bed. If I used my crutches in a certain way, it was painless to drag my leg along as long as I didn't try to lift it. So, I decided to go to work anyway and had to sit my way up the stairs backward, one step at a time, pushing with my good leg. My husband and friends were shocked, but I couldn't let an accident, as a result of my hobby, interfere with the service and responsibility I felt towards the Lord's work. I healed quickly, however, and eagerly resumed my riding after about eight weeks as soon as the doctor said I was mended.

As time went on, I had to come to terms with the fact that I had begun my sport totally ignorant of the expens-

es involved in learning to ride a trained rental horse, not
to mention the boots and breeches I needed. Riding once
a week was hard enough on the budget, but now twice a
week was a real stretch. I struggled with trying to reconcile
my newfound heart's desire with the limited financial re-
sources available. That was also the beginning of a tension
that would drive me to my knees before the Lord.

Frank and I talked about it and prayed together trying
to decide what the Lord would have me do. Despite Frank's
love for me and consistently generous spirit, he had to lay
out the cold, hard facts and help me realize that our household budget didn't include my extracurricular activities.
The decision was difficult for both of us to make.

However, with tears in my eyes and an ache in my
heart, I gave up my riding lessons with the confidence that
God would honor my being submissive to my husband's
counsel with the right heart attitude. I knew through Scripture that God would direct me through my husband, and
I was not afraid of God's will. On the contrary, I looked
forward to what He would do next with complete trust
and anticipation. As it says in 1 Peter 3:6, *"Just as Sarah
obeyed Abraham, calling him lord, and you have become
her children if you do what is right without being frightened by any fear."* We decided to give any extra money we
saved from the lessons to the Lord's work, trusting the Lord
for His perfect will. And we were confident of another
biblical principle: you can't out-give God! As Jesus taught

in the well-known Sermon on the Mount, *"Give, and it will be given to you. They will pour into your lap a good measure—pressed down, shaken together, and running over. For by your standard of measure it will be measured to you in return"* (Luke 6:38).

Shortly thereafter, I decided to take an inexpensive three-month course called "Horse Husbandry" at the local community college so that I could at least learn about horses academically. I learned everything I could about the magnificent animal—good and bad. At that point, I had a pretty rough idea of the expense involved in owning a horse, and the class taught me the responsibility of caring for such a majestic but fragile and almost totally dependent creature. Yet, I still suffered with the wanting of one. I saw a program on television with a herd of horses running across a meadow and cried out in my heart, *Lord, if I could have just one of those!* It got to the point that I knew was not honoring in my desire to trust the Lord, so I finally went to my knees privately in my bedroom and turned my longing over to God. I prayed that if He was not going to fulfill the desire, would He please just take it away? Fearing that fulfilling my desire was too selfish and complicated, I pleaded, "Lord, I know how kind and generous you are, but please don't even think about *giving* me a horse. Because even *if* you *give* me one, I can't afford to pay board or buy feed, or shoes, or vet bills, not to mention lessons! So, *please, just take this desire away."* When I dried my eyes, I felt like a hundred-pound weight had been lifted off my shoulders. I truly was willing to give Him my desire to ride or own a horse. From that point on, I was able to rest in the fact that God heard my prayer and would do what was best, and I would just enjoy horses from a distance.

One thing the Horse Husbandry class could do was to give me hands-on experience in handling a horse through periodic field trips to nearby ranches. We had sessions when we practiced brushing a horse, learned what tool to use to clean the hooves, etc., and we had a farrier class where we actually had an opportunity to hit with a hammer a *real* nail into a *real* horseshoe while on the *real* horse's hoof!

While our class attended a show-jumping event at the Los Angeles Equestrian Center (LAEC) in Burbank, I walked over to the stables in the back with a classmate, Marty, and met a new acquaintance, Barbara. She was the owner of a string of the most beautiful performance horses I had ever seen. She had almost one of every breed and color! I was in awe, gawking at her equine treasures. Marty and I made a quick tour and started to leave.

"Oh!" I blurted out, clenching my teeth and fists, "I wish I could just hang around here on a regular basis and be near these beautiful horses!"

"Well, why don't you ask?" Marty suggested. But I was afraid—afraid I would be intruding, afraid Barbara would think me a pest. "All she can say is no. Come on, I'll go with you," Marty offered.

"Oh Lord, give me courage," I prayed audibly, looking up to the heavens. "Lord, thy will be done," Marty wisely added. With that and Marty's moral support, we turned on our heels and walked back to the tack room where Barbara was preparing buckets of carrots for the afternoon feeding.

"Uh, excuse me. I was just here admiring your beautiful horses and—well, I sort of have an idea," I offered timidly.

"What's that?" she queried.

"Well, you said that you come to the barn really early in the morning, right? Like about 6:00 a.m.?"

"Right." She looked at me quizzically.

"Would it be possible for me to come at 6:00 a.m. and just hang around and learn as much as I can?" I felt I was begging after all. But to my surprise, her suspicion turned into a warm acceptance.

"Sure!" she grinned. "You come anytime, and I'll have my groom show you what to do."

"Great! I'll be here." *Wow, she went for it!* I thought to myself. And she didn't seem to think I was a pest—she even responded like she liked the idea. Marty gave me a big smile, and I virtually skipped out of there with Marty in tow. That was a Sunday afternoon.

I was so excited that I felt like a kid on Christmas Eve.

I wanted to go the following Monday morning but forced myself to wait until Wednesday morning. Since I lived thirty miles away from the barn, I had to get up at 4:30 a.m. to get myself dressed for barn work and also prepared for office work later. Everything I would need to change into was packed, and I hit the road. I was there by 6:00 a.m. sharp!

My time there at the barn was wonderful! The groom put a brush in my hand, stood me at the horse's side, and said, "Brush the same direction the hair goes!" She showed me how to tie slipknots, pick hooves, wipe runny noses, and rinse off sweaty horses. I got all the "hands-on" I wanted! And I gladly came back on Friday—at 6:00 a.m. for more of the same.

I drank in everything I could and watched closely to learn how to groom, saddle up, and bridle several horses with their various personalities and idiosyncrasies. Each horse had its own special bridle, and often the bits weren't the same. A seasoned, well-trained horse could go with a simple snaffle bit—the most common type of English bit. The younger ones would sometimes wear a thinner bit that was more "severe" than the snaffle and would keep their attention, or the well-trained show horses would wear a double bridle with two bits to reinforce the difficult movements they were practicing. Proper communication from the rider's gentle hands to the horse's mouth was paramount. But I'm getting ahead of myself.

"Arabest Annelia"—As Though She Were Yours

The second day I was there, that Friday, Barbara rode back to the barn and dismounted. "So, Pat, how often are you planning on coming?" She questioned.

"Well, I figured every Monday, Wednesday, and Friday morning from about 6:00-7:30 if that's okay with you."

"Would you like to ride?" she asked.

I went numb. Shock, I think. *What? Ride? Me?* Honestly, it hadn't even occurred to me—really! I didn't know people would let other people ride their horses. I just wanted to hang around, to touch, to brush! *Ride? Me?* That's what was racing through my head. But I had to remain cool because I was on the verge of happy tears. So, I sort of played my toe in the dirt and quietly said, "Sure. Who would I ride?"

"You can ride Annie" (this equine friend I hadn't met yet).

"Who's Annie?" I asked.

"Let me show you," she said, and she walked me down a few stalls. "That's Annie. She's an Arabian mare, and you can ride her every time you come—as often as you like. In fact, *I want you to treat her as though she were your own horse.* Let me show you her tack," at which point she walked me back to the tack room and pointed out Annie's saddle and bridle and grooming kit.

More numbness. More shock. "Really?! Gosh, thanks, Barbara!" My head was spinning.

It was time to go, and I had to change clothes to look feminine again to go to work. But I had a horse I could ride! Anytime I wanted! *As though she were your own horse*—the words kept ringing over and over in my head.

I climbed into my car and drove on a cloud to work. I could hardly wait to get to my office and call Frank to tell him that God had found a way! He had done it! He had found a way to *give* me a horse without really giving it to me—and I didn't have to pay for board, or feed, or vet, or shoes! I didn't have to rent it or lease it or buy it! (An exact answer to my very specific prayer!) And He gave it to me *"Exceedingly, abundantly beyond all that [I could] ask or think"* (Ephesians 3:20). Annie came with saddle and bridle and all the equipment I would ever need, plus a groom to ask a million questions of and other riders to ride with. And she wasn't just any backyard nag; she was *Arabest Annelia,* "Annie," a beautiful, 15.2 hand, chestnut, 99 percent Egyptian Arabian mare. She had the typical Arabian concave dish face and a pretty little white snip on her muzzle as well as a beautiful, long tail, and she was to be "as though she were yours." Frank and I both wept with joy at God's overt goodness in answering my prayer through Barbara's unexpected, thoughtful generosity, and I was reminded of one of my favorite verses: Psalm 37:4-5, *"Delight yourself in the Lord and He will give you the desires of your heart. Trust also in Him and He will do it."*

I was also reminded of a very valuable Scriptural principle—that when we are willing to give something up to the Lord, He often gives it back, as in the story of Abraham offering up Isaac, his *"only son, whom you love"* (Genesis 22:2). As long as Abraham was willing to give him up, God did not require it of him because He knew what was in Abraham's heart by the depth of his sacrifice (verses 9-17), and God said, *"For now I know that you fear God, since you have not withheld...from Me"* (verse 12).

Whenever I come to a point in my spiritual walk with God, when I wonder about His love for me or His care over the tiniest desire of my heart, the words that come to my mind are, *Remember the horse!* Remember Annie. Remember how God answered your prayer and gave to you abundantly beyond what you ever imagined—and how that prayer still continues to be answered to this day. Remember the horse! Remember God's wondrous acts! *"I will remember the works of the LORD; ...I will also meditate on all Your work, and talk of Your deeds!"* (Psalm 77:11-12, NKJV).

Reality Sets In

For the next six months, my energy ran on pure enthusiasm. I got up at 4:30 a.m. on Mondays, Wednesdays, and Fridays and even went out to the barn most Saturdays. I groomed and rode Annie to my heart's content, but it wasn't long before I realized that what I was doing was really difficult—getting up very early, packing toiletries and a change of clothes, driving a long distance, and riding a hot-blooded horse who was a lamb on the ground but a lion under saddle for a green rider like me. I had a full workout even before I went to the office to put in another eight hours at a fast-paced ministry to which I was committed and was my life's priority, but was laden with its many demands and stresses. Then I would drag home, have dinner with Frank, do a few chores and fall into bed.

As time went on, Frank was so supportive of my vocation and my avocation (my riding) that he began to learn his way around the kitchen to help take the pressure off me since, by that time, he was enjoying an early semi-retirement. And after a dozen years of being married by then, we both began to realize his hidden culinary talents! Many nights we would share a delicious meal together that he had cooked! (My suspicion that I had married a wonderfully kind, gentle, and loving man had, once again, been confirmed!).

With Annie, I learned the most important lesson of just being able to stay in the saddle! Nothing compares to consistent saddle time, and, for a green rider like I was, Annie was almost feistier and more energetic than I could handle. One day, I remember looking up from the dirt after being thrown and thinking how pretty she was as I watched her galloping off without me.

The particular equestrian discipline followed by our barn was called dressage (pronounced "dress-*ajh*"). Of importance to suggest is that the best way for a green rider to learn dressage is on a seasoned horse. And the best way for a green horse to learn is to have a seasoned rider. Well, here I was: a green rider on a green horse! Annie didn't know the first thing about dressage, or at least if she did, she never let on. She was an Arabian—and in her horsy mind were visions of herself racing across the Arabian Desert with colorful silk sashes around her neck flashing in the wind. At least, that's what I envisioned as I attempted to ride her and keep my seat. The more I watched my friends ride their dressage movements, the more I longed to be able to do the same with Annie. One brave soul attempted to give us backyard lessons, and we were certainly a challenge. But I loved every bit of it and loved Annie to bits! One thing was for sure; I kept her spit-shined and polished. I could groom her like a champ!

Barbara became a quick friend. She was so attentive and very kind to me in my enthusiasm for riding Annie, and that included allowing me to be in a photoshoot she had arranged for some of her show horses. Thankfully, I had ascertained show clothes because, during my previous very elementary training, I had been in a beginners' "flat class" where the riders simply walked, trotted, or cantered their horses without maneuvering any jumps. I had won that class which thrilled me to the core—you would have thought I had won a million dollars; I was so happy.

Nevertheless, I was at least prepared costume-wise for the photoshoot even though Annie and I were far from ready for any serious showing.

But Barbara took me under her wing. I was able to go to a few of her shows when she rode her classes and assist her as best I could. I was like a kid in a candy shop, and I think Barbara got a kick out of my enthusiasm over any and all of it. In fact, a birthday of mine came along, and Barbara instructed Frank and me to meet her at a particular restaurant. Upon arrival, I found a dozen of my new riding compatriots sitting around a long table with a huge cake in the center of it displaying an icing rendition of a horse's head, saying, "Happy Birthday, Pat." I was stunned and overjoyed. I had never had a birthday party like that in my life, and Barbara made sure I was showered with gifts—all horse-related: jackets and riding shirts with horse logos, socks, horse charms, trinkets—I was in horsey-heaven and felt the love orchestrated by my new friends. At times, she would even take me to the local tack shop where any horse-lover would drool at all the gorgeous equipment and outfits, and she would let me pick something special. She knew my pennies were limited, so she bought me my first pair of white dressage show breeches, making sure they fit just right. Now all I had to do was practice, practice, practice!

We went to other shows, exhibitions, and upper-level training clinics too. In fact, many of the Olympic riding contenders were located in California because the climate allowed them to train all year. We saw clinics conducted by Hilda Gurney, who won the Team Bronze medal in the 1984 Summer Games on her American Thoroughbred, Keen, right there at the Los Angeles Equestrian Center where I was riding! Hilda was Barbara's personal friend and trainer, and I was in awe of the auspicious company in which I found myself.

As I met other new friends, we also drove south of LA to watch Steffan Peters at his San Diego ranch conduct clinics for competition hopefuls. Years later, in 1996, Steffan, who became a three-time Olympian, won the Team Bronze medal at the Atlanta Games (which Frank and I were privileged and thrilled to personally attend and witness) on the beautiful Floriano.

Then, there were clinics conducted by Gunter Seidel who was a German native who moved to the US in 1985. He also aided the US in winning the Team Bronze medal at three consecutive Olympic Games with different horses, beginning alongside Steffan at the 1996 Atlanta Games with his majestic grey, Graf George.

A Spiritual Stepping Stone

But what had begun as fun with the horses, the Lord was going to use to teach me spiritual and physical discipline and commitment. I was very cognizant of the fact that God had given me a gift and had answered my prayer in a magnanimous way, not just for my enjoyment but also for His glory. I knew that I couldn't take His gift lightly, and I couldn't be a flake who didn't follow through to my new friends at the barn who, by this time, knew that I was a professing Christian. I was grateful to God for His loving kindness to me, grateful to Barbara for her generosity, and desirous of being a good testimony for my Lord by being faithful and not giving up when the going got tough. Plus, I was surrounded by other new friends whom I grew to love that didn't know the Lord personally, and I wanted to nurture those relationships. So, I kept on keeping on.

CHAPTER 2

Fahrenheit

The Schoolmaster

"Because of the tender mercy of our God, With
which the Sunrise from on high shall visit us,
To shine upon those who sit in darkness
and the shadow of death, To guide our
feet into the way of peace."
(Luke 1:78-79)

After about two years of Annie training me not to fall off, another horse became available, and Barbara offered him to me as my next mount. (With mixed emotions on my part, Annie moved on to another barn.) His name was Fahrenheit ("Fefe" for short— every horse in the barn had a nickname). He was a 17.2 hand "gentle giant" (quite big compared to Annie's 15.2 hands)! He was a chestnut-colored, German Oldenburg gelding with a wonderful disposition. I had watched Barbara ride him and, with my new interest in dressage, was impressed with how he moved. In fact, he had won First Level Horse of the Year with Barbara's accomplished riding and had also been shown at Fourth Level. Because of arthritis, however, she said he would never be able to compete any higher than that. So, typically thoughtful Barbara decided that Fefe would be a good school horse for—guess who?—Me!

Was he ever! This was my formal introduction to dressage, and free lessons came with the horse! Was I surprised? Yes, and grateful beyond words, but God had it all planned and was in complete control. The Bible says in Jeremiah 29:11, *"'For I know the plans that I have for you,' declares the Lord, 'plans for welfare and not for calamity, to give you a future and a hope.'"* It continued to boggle my mind that not only did God demonstrate His love to me by providing a horse for me in the first place, but now He was providing an unspoken prayer – a thought – a wish: dressage lessons! I knew that in response to His sovereign goodness to me, I had to remain faithful to do the very best that I could in order to glorify Him and make His goodness known to others through my life and through my riding—somehow.

I rode Fefe almost every morning, and we had a lesson once a week. Our onsite trainer taught me much, and Fefe was willing and obedient. He didn't seem to mind having a green rider like me on his back. If I even slightly pushed the right "buttons" to give him close to the right signal to do something, he did it for me. What a horse! I was finally ready for my first show, and we took two blue ribbons in a "Green as Grass" class, which was the bottom of the rung in a dressage show! I was so proud of him, but I'm sure he was prouder of me!

Barbara tightening our girth.

Fefe's perfect Blue Ribbon "bend."

~~~~~.

As time went on, I was told that Fefe's only idiosyncra-sy was that if something really spooked him (which wasn't often), he would bolt. Being so big and strong, it was hard to stop him once he got started running. I hadn't experi-enced that personally and hoped I never would.

My baptism by fire came at a Reiner Klimke Clinic. Mr. Klimke was a highly respected, six-time Olympic Gold medal winner for Germany in dressage, my dressage idol at-a-distance, and the finest rider and trainer in the history of dressage in the opinions of many worldwide competi-tors. Germany, as a matter of fact, was illustrious for being

the country to excel in the mastery of the sport. One of my
secret wishes was to someday go to Germany to train with
him personally. As Norman Vincent Peale put it many years
ago, "Shoot for the moon. Even if you miss, you'll land
among the stars." But I knew one had to be good, really
good, and have a healthy, athletic horse with great potential
worth tens or even hundreds of thousands of dollars (literally). That, of course, brought me back to reality. However,
one can imagine my excitement when Barbara arranged for
me to ride Fefe in a workshop conducted by Mr. Klimke's
associate who had flown in from Germany, which was not
only a real honor for me but also a nerve-wracking thought.
Evidently, judging by what happened next, Fefe felt my
nervousness just as easily as he could feel my self-assur-
ance if I had any!

Several of us were riding in the arena, and each horse's
movement was being scrutinized. The point of the clinic
was to demonstrate what to look for in a dressage horse in
front of an audience of eager spectators wanting to learn. If
that wasn't intimidating enough, the movement of the horse
totally depended upon the expertise (or not) of the rider
(me!). Added to that, the clinician's voice was carried by a
microphone into squawking portable speakers. His voice
bounced off the Equidome ceiling of the Equestrian Center, and the speakers in two of the corners attacked Fefe's
confidence every time we passed by. It was more than he
could handle, and he began to become more than I thought
I could handle. I was attempting to keep him moving at a

nice comfortable working trot to which I could easily post. After ten, very long, seemingly eternal minutes of subtly battling to keep him under control, which wore down my bravery second by second (it was more a battle of the minds), he began to passage (*pas- 'saj*) which is more of a high-stepping collected trot. It is a natural movement horses can do, especially when particularly alerted by something, and a show horse like Fefe was trained by Barbara to give that movement upon command when she had practiced fourth level with him. Wikipedia has a simple to understand definition:

> Passage is a movement seen in upper-level dressage, in which the horse performs a highly elevated and *extremely powerful trot*. The horse is very collected and *moves with great impulsion*. The passage *differs from the working,* medium, collected, and extended trot *(italics mine)*.

Needless to say, I had not been trained to ride Fefe in the passage; therefore, I naturally had not asked him to perform it! The rider is trained to *sit* this bouncy action, but my self-preservation instinct caused me to keep posting since it was still sort of a trot! But I knew I was in trouble—he was passaging because he was getting more and more upset. Sure enough, Fefe took off in a gallop and headed for the edge of the dressage arena. He jumped over the poles, and I lost all poise as I lost control of him. It was terrifying... and humiliating.

Fefe made a sharp left turn and headed back up the other side. I was in such shock; I didn't have a clue what I should do and, strangely, didn't try anymore to rein him in. After the previous ten minutes, he had won the mind game, so the reins seemed useless to me. I looked down at that huge neck which was pumping like the wheels of a locomotive and just as powerful with the blowing of his hot breath and the thunder of his massive hooves. It seemed to last forever. Fefe turned again, and I could see us headed straight for another horse and rider. We could hit them broadside. *Does Fefe see them, or is he blinded by fear?* My anxious mind shouted!

I belted out the loudest prayer I have ever prayed: "Lord Jesus, help me!" At that precise moment, Fefe made another sharp turn and began running a little more slowly along the wall, which gave me the idea to bail off, hoping to grab the wall before I fell off or had a major wreck with the other riders in the area. Scraping my gloved hands down the wall helped to break my fall, but I still landed face down in the dirt rather than on my feet, which added to my humiliation in front of 250 people and Reiner Klimke's assistant! The minute I came off, however, Fefe slowed, and friends were able to grab his reins to stop him. I got up off the ground, spitting the dirt from my mouth, and stayed down on one knee, with my arms spread out at my sides to show the crowd I was all right. Everyone applauded in goodwill despite my mishap, which helped to salve my bruised self-respect. But I had no doubt that the Lord had protected me, Fefe, and everyone else in the arena from injury. All I broke were a few fingernails—and my pride.

As we walked out of the arena, people were so kind. One nice lady who had been in the stands came up to console me, saying that she was glad I had not been injured, but innocently making a side comment: "I've never seen anyone post the passage before." Little did she know that was because I had no idea what I was doing, but I never let on to that fact! Nevertheless, I was able to share how I had called on the Lord and how He had heard my cry. Even in a frightening situation like that, God was glorified because I was able to experience and testify that He promises, *"I will never desert you nor will I ever forsake you,"* as the Bible says in Hebrews 13:5. Even though riders are encouraged to get right back onto a horse that has thrown them, lest the fear take hold and they determine never to climb aboard again, I didn't and called it a day, albeit a disappointing and embarrassing one. We just walked Fefe back to his stall.

It surprised me that night how traumatized I had been by the whole ordeal. I could visualize in my dreams the powerfully pumping neck I had stared at in disbelief and the sound of the pounding of his huge feet as he galloped uncontrollably. I soothed my mind with a comforting verse from the well-known hymn, "How Firm A Foundation" (author unknown), referencing the Scripture in Isaiah 41:10, which had become one of my favorites:

Fear not, I am with thee; O be not dismayed;
For I am thy God, and will still give thee aid; I'll
strengthen thee, help thee, and cause thee to stand,
Upheld by My righteous, omnipotent hand.

By the next day, however, I overcame my fear with my
trainer by our side on the ground, reassuring me that it was
a completely unusual situation for Fefe and we would be
fine in our lesson to follow. I was also reminded that Fefe
had also been traumatized, which is why he bolted. Now I
had an opportunity to comfort him. My compassion for him
helped me to overcome my own emotions. We were fine
in our lesson, and I was grateful for this sweet animal that
would not have wanted to hurt me in any way or even scare
me. As many barns will post on their walls, "Ride at your
own risk." There is always a risk involved around horses
who often are not aware of their own strength, but the temperament of a horse like Fefe's was a blessing 99 percent of
the time. We became great partners.

We continued to ride and train for about a year and a
half until he bowed a tendon in some deep mud after a rainstorm. I nursed him for several months to no avail, wrapping his injured leg daily while his big frame stood still in
a small stall, not being allowed to put any additional strain
on that tendon. But his huge size and heavy weight were
not boding well in his favor, and Barbara decided he would
be better off being put out to pasture where he could heal
in his own timing. He was in the prime of his life, and we

hoped this would be a good solution. Another friend and I trailered him out to a ranch that had large pastures, and it was difficult leaving him there because it was so far out that I knew I would be unable to visit him. He was never able to make a comeback, however, became ill many months later with kidney failure and, sadly, had to be put down.

In fact, Fefe died about a week after my mother died. Frank and I had flown to Detroit for her funeral. We spent the week, along with my three sisters, going through the house we had grown up in, attempting to determine what to do with all of its contents. While I was there, Barbara called to notify me about Fefe's demise. I was devastated, already being tender-hearted over my mother's passing. There was lingering grief because this was only six months after our father died. I also had to put down one of my sweet dogs *and* a cat earlier. Having lost both parents within six months of each other, with the added heartache of three precious pets, it was a heavy-hearted time, and I clung to the Lord in desperation for His comfort. A favorite hymn came to mind at my time of grief and unwanted changes in my life. It's called "Be Still My Soul." One powerful verse goes like this:

> Be still my soul! The Lord is on thy side;
> Bear patiently the cross of grief or pain;
> Leave to thy God to order and provide;
> In every change He faithful will remain.
> Be still my soul! thy best, thy heavenly Friend

Thro' thorny ways leads to a joyful end.[i]

Sometimes I have to remind myself of this truth when
I go through difficult times in life. If God cares enough to
send His grace to comfort me over the death of a loved one
or even the loss of an animal precious to me, won't He dis-
play His great compassion and mercy over other situations
that weigh heavily on my heart? When life throws an un-
certain future at us, or mountainous hurdles that are beyond
our control, or the knowledge of our own ugly sinfulness
that is ever before us, we can be assured that God cares and
comes to our rescue. The Bible says that not one sparrow
*"...is forgotten before God. Indeed, the very hairs of your
head are all numbered. Do not fear; you are more valuable
than many sparrows"* (Luke 12:6-7).

So, Fefe introduced me to the beauty and discipline
of dressage, and the Lord used him to get me started in
that specific direction in my riding. Being goal-oriented
and competitive by nature, I was always striving to do my
best. Being a Christian, I was eager to be excellent for the
Lord's sake. Dressage challenged me to do both and, when
the horse is just as willing, there's no feeling like it in the
world. The teamwork of two minds and two bodies melded
together in such a way so as to present one graceful unit
performing equestrian ballet was one of the most satisfying
physical endeavors I had ever attempted. God's power was
manifested over and over to me not only at the time when
He saved me from injury at the Klimke Clinic, but moment

by moment as I would pray and struggle to learn the correct "aids" in this very precise, demanding, but beautiful sport. I often thought of Hebrews 12:11:

> *All discipline for the moment seems not to be joyful, but sorrowful; yet to those who have been trained by it, afterwards it yields the peaceful fruit of righteousness.*

Fefe was not meant to be my champion, but he was a wonderful schoolmaster, for which I will ever be grateful.

CHAPTER 3

Dressage
The Wonder of It All

"Also if anyone competes as an athlete,
He does not win the prize
Unless he competes according to the rules."
(2 Timothy 2:5)

The word is derived from the French verb "dresser," which simply means "schooling" or "to train." For over 2,000 years, dressage has been a combination of art and technique, training the horse to perform natural movements on command but with a combination of artistic flair and technical control while maintaining the natural stride and balance of the horse. To me, it's like dancing—a ballet performed by a duo, one human and one equine, when a horse and rider think and move as one. The intense demands of the sport are imperceptible to those who have never studied or ridden it—every gesture, every subtle signal, even every thought—is perceived by the horse as a command to obey in the ever-elusive quest for total harmony between horse and rider. The high-spirited beauty of the horse's gaits is controlled by the rider with "aids" that can make or break the quality of the desired movement or even jeopardize the movement itself. There is a striving for perfection, a faultless execution that is ultimately never reached. Most upper-level riders admit that the more they learn, the more they need to learn. It's an elegant discipline. It's a journey, a relationship, a oneness. It's incredible. And that's not just my single opinion. Danielle Casalett, a fifteen-year-old junior rider from Granite Bay, California, put it this way:

> Dressage is one of the hardest sports in the equestrian field. You can never expect where you will be day to day. Some days are the best ever and other days are not so good. This is what I love about it. I have competed in other equestrian disciplines, but dressage gives me the most rewarding feeling. My love for dressage is like no other. It means waking up at 5:00 a.m. to clean stalls before I go to school. Giving everything up to train is what truly dedicates me to the sport of dressage. It has taught me patience, discipline and humility. Dressage is my passion.[ii]

As I said before, I had a long way to go to catch up with the younger generation!

It might be helpful to the reader at this point to understand more of the details of dressage: what it is, how it works, and what it takes to perform. The beginnings of "classical" dressage go all the way back to the Middle Ages using the horse as a war machine, but reaching into the period of the Renaissance as logically trained horses showed their prowess and that of their masters. Eventually reaching into the Olympics in 1912 for enlisted men (no women), it took another forty years before civilian riders could finally compete in the auspicious games. These civilians now range from both genders of any age through any walk of life or vocation (including secretaries like me). Whoever we are, we find a common bond in our love of the majestic equine and the challenge of finding the perfect aids that bring out the best performance of horse and rider as a team.

It really doesn't matter the breed or color, even size or age of a dressage-sport horse; however, in the upper levels, as the movements become more challenging, most serious competitors prefer larger breeds, such as warm bloods like Hanoverian, Dutch, or Trakehner. Some hot-blooded horses like Thoroughbreds or Arabians are able to compete as well; however, their temperament might cause them to feel claustrophobic in the ring as they are being trained to "collect" or compress their frame rather than stretch out or move swiftly. Whatever the breed, they need to be athletic and light on their feet. Age is a factor if the more difficult movements place too much stress on the joints of a horse prone to arthritis. *The Spectator's Guide to Dressage* compiled by the Los Angeles Dressage Committee notes, "Exceptional basic paces—walk, trot, and canter—together with a good temperament and sound conformation are what riders look for in a potential dressage horse." [iii]

As I was learning along with Fefe, I enjoyed what the

young riders were teaching me! In a "Meet the Juniors" article from the California Dressage Society newsletter, another junior rider, Kelsey Bullock, a sixteen-year-old from Danville, California, shared her thoughts:

> My favorite part of dressage was the complete elegance of the sport. I loved the way horse and rider work together silently as one... I understood that it wasn't silent beauty all the time. Dressage means hard work and perfection. Perhaps my favorite part of dressage is how the rider sits pretty on the horse and gives unidentifiable commands. It seems as if the rider is giving all the credit to the horse, even though we all know it takes a lot of work to be a dressage rider.[iv]

Of course, reading a wonderful story like Kelsey's reminded me—here she was, "sweet-sixteen" and already well on her way in her pursuit of this beautiful sport while I, a forty-something, was just starting out! Was I chagrinned and intimidated by these talented youngsters? Absolutely yes! But I studied, and we trained and, in the final analysis, did well!

The 100 percent score is virtually unattainable even by the best of the best; however, in 2014, British competitor Neil McIntosh on JazzBeat scored the perfect 100 percent mark for a *Materiale* test at the Ottawa Dressage Festival in Canada (May 30-June 1).

A *Materiale* class is taken from the German class-es (and name), and it is just to judge on the basic gaits and general impressions (and sometimes con-formation) of the young/prospect horse for future training. Of course, the rider is highly experienced (Internet article, *The Chronicle of the Horse*).

In my meager beginnings, my scores only ranged in the mid-fifties. Gladly, with time and training, we did improve to mid-sixties which were considered acceptable, and I have several first-place blue ribbons to show for it!

Watching Barbara and the other more experienced rid-ers in my barn prepare for their shows and, finally stepping out on my own, it became paramount that the spit-shined presentation of horse, tack, and rider was almost just as important as riding the test itself. I learned to braid manes and polish tack and boots. Also, a warm-up ride prior to the test was crucial in order to stretch and prepare the horse's muscles for the equine "weightlifting" routine he was about to perform. He truly becomes a gymnast. I found that warming up in an arena with several other dressage riders warming up at the same time was a challenge in and of it-self! They all seemed to be at much higher levels than I was judging from their horses' upper-level movements. The last thing I wanted to do was collide with one of them as I at-tempted to concentrate on my own more basic routine!

Shown below is a typical full-sized dressage arena—twenty by sixty meters—with large, visible markers at the entrance, along the two long sides, and also at the far short side. There are also unseen markers down the middle to coincide with the instructions of whatever test is being taken. Of course, the horse doesn't see them, but the rider and the judges know they are there. "X" marks the spot right in the middle, where the horse and rider are supposed to make a perfectly straight and square halt (that is the goal) after entering the arena at "A."

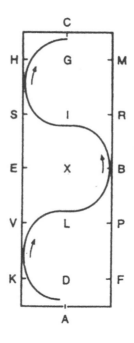

I was watching a friend at a show one day who had just entered the arena at "A" and halted at "X." She lowered her right arm while holding the reins with her left hand, bowed her head, and saluted the judges. At that precise moment, her horse needed to urinate! There was no way, in his squatted position, that she could urge him forward into the impressive trot the judges were expecting, so she just had to wait. No one can blame a horse for nature calling, so after a number of seconds which felt like an eternity, she urged him forward into the called-for trot. The test proceeded nicely until it came time to ride the "diagonal." That is accomplished by riding, for example, from the letter "M" (see top right of the arena) kitty-corner across the whole arena, through "X," meeting up with the letter "K" (at the bottom left). The diagonal is usually ridden at an extended trot where the horse stretches out his stride without picking up tempo but actually covers more ground. Naturally, in a horse's way of thinking, when you see a puddle on the ground (at "X" where he'd peed), you don't want to step in it—so you jump it! That, of course, did not bode well with the judges' scoring of that movement, especially when they had to eventually come back the other way from "F" to "H" and jump "X" again! Everyone got a great laugh over it nonetheless, even though the competitor did not receive the score she had hoped.

The Guide explains further about the classes offered in order of difficulty:

> ...Training Level, First, Second, Third, Fourth Levels, the Prix St. Georges, Intermediaire I, Intermediaire II, and Grand Prix.

> Within the Grand Prix level are the Grand Prix de Dressage, the test used to determine team medals

at the Olympics, and the Grand Prix Special, the test used to determine the individual medals. It is in these tests that we see the most spectacular movements: Piaffe, the highly collected, elevated trot in place; Passage, the suspended trot in slow-motion; Pirouette, a rhythmic turning in place at the walk and canter; Half Pass, a forward and sideways movement at the trot and canter where the horse crosses his legs; Flying Change, a skipping type movement at the canter where the horse changes his leading leg every fourth, third, second, and finally, at every stride.[v]

The challenge, of course, is for the rider to earn the horse's trust with consistent training so that the movements noted above are performed on command without resistance, even while carrying well over a hundred pounds on his back. Even though these movements are natural to the horse, yet the Guide goes on to say, "The trust of the horse and the harmony which makes this possible are a tribute to the rider's ability and the horse's generosity." [vi]

The Freestyle to Music, sometimes known as Musical Kur, became my favorite to watch and my highest goal. It was a ride put to music with the movements and tempo choreographed by the rider and is usually the favorite test for everyone to watch. But the thrill is not for the spectator alone, as depicted by this young rider and essay winner, Brooke Lemke, entitled "The Gift of Dance." It is so beautifully described that it's worth the read:

> As she stood perfectly still with her partner, she took several deep breaths preparing her for what was to be the dance of her lifetime. With the sign from the judge, she calmly and collectively picked up the reins and held her partner. She raised her hand for the music to begin. Without hesitation, they proceeded dancing together.
>
> Ever since his birth she knew that he was the one, her partner 'til death. The trust between the two was apparent in their dance. She could make the slightest move to ask for something and he gave it. The grace and poise they possessed were mystifying. Her shadbelly *(uniform of top-hat and tails [ital. mine])* flowed over the saddle and landed on her partner's translucent copper coat. His energy was contained yet projected to the point that he would suspend the two of them in the air for seconds. Every move matched perfectly to each beat of the music. The two of them were so tuned into each other and to the music that the crowd and judge didn't exist. They were no longer competing for the championship or for the highest points. They were dancing because they wanted to, not because they had to.
>
> This was more than another dance. They were two beings from two different worlds coming togeth-

er as one body. There her seat met his back and it looked as though they were connected. These two worlds collided for a few minutes and they were no longer "beauty and the beast," they were one. They had one body, one spirit and one heart. They accomplished the goal of dancing together that so many people could only dream of. This was more than another art or sport, it was a gift. It was a gift of dance and love that only their creator could provide and only a few could master. This gift is Dressage.

When the music came to an end, she took one final breath. Even though the dance was over, the memory would live on forever. Tears swelled in her eyes as she hugged her partner whispering the words, "Thank you, I'll never forget this."[vii]

As I began to work in my training to get to the point of being ready to "dance" with my horse, I never could get the above literary picture out of my mind. One of my less successful attempts is described in a later chapter. However, it was so fun to attempt to ride to music. The Musical Kur combines the passion for the sport with the artistic beauty of the movements, enhanced by the carefully selected musical scores. No two tests are ever alike, and World Championships can be won or lost by the choreography performed by the horse and rider team. It was all up to the judges!

I found dressage very appealing for several reasons. To

me, it was similar to the disciplines of figure skating—as precise as making perfectly round circles, not ovals—which takes much more effort than imagined. Of course, to certain onlookers who don't pursue this sport, the lower levels are like "watching paint dry." Training and First Levels, especially, consist of roundness and straightness, obedient halts, and a walk, trot, or canter on queue. However, as the geometry of the sport becomes more and more complicated from level to level, the onlookers eventually have to pick their jaws up from the ground when they see a gorgeous, thousand-pound animal literally skipping across the arena, seemingly of its own accord, with imperceptible aids from the rider that are practically telepathic. Eat your heart out!

I will never forget the rush I felt the first time, after months of practice when my horse just *knew* I wanted to make a turn even before I gave the command (or so I thought). Truth be told, our own thoughts are so powerfully in tune with our own bodies that thinking something might cause a response to the smallest muscle, albeit unbeknownst to us. But the horse seems to know it. Sometimes, just a turning of the head will lead him in that direction. Looking up and straight ahead is very important to keep him straight, rather than the tendency to look down at the horse's neck and head (which we are always trying to keep "rounded" or on the bit). Even an ever-so-slight shift of weight in the saddle sends him to one side or the other. We might conclude it is telepathic but, to the horse's sense of feel, while carrying our weight, being in tune with all of nature around him, including the "animal" on his back, he is very much infused with the signals we send to him known or unknown to ourselves. And to get the two of them in sync at the same time is beyond thrilling. That's where very precise training for the rider becomes paramount, no matter how many years it takes.

Again, the Spectator's Guide explains:

> When a horse is working "with" the rider, not just "for" the rider, has achieved a harmony with him, and can perform movements that demand great athleticism, then dressage is a source of great excitement and wonderful memories for rider, judge, and spectator alike.[viii]

I couldn't have said it better myself. Oh, the wonder of it all!

CHAPTER 4

Liponio ~
A Blanket of Peace

"Save me from the lion's mouth;
And from the horns of the wild oxen!
You have answered me."
(Psalm 22:21, NKJV)

After Fahrenheit's death, God remained faithful as Barbara provided another temporary mount for me by the name of Liponio. I had the privilege of riding him for about six months to assist his trainer by exercising him. He was a beautiful, white, Andalusian stallion and helped instill much confidence in me since I couldn't believe that I was actually riding a stallion for the first time!

I had heard several stories, true or false, about stallions—they can't be near any other horse, male or female. I pictured them as hot, snorting, whinnying mounts that have a mind of their own and the muscle to back it up. One false move and the rider has been outwitted and out bullied by a heavy-breathing, pulsating ton of war-machine. But not Liponio. He was a big puppy dog. Oh, I had to keep our distance from other horses all right, but he never fought me on it. In fact, he was downright cooperative.

The Andalusian breed originated in Andalusia, Spain. They actually were used for war, and their cavalry officers were master equestrians who taught these horses the art of using their natural gaits as weapons in battle, including what's called "airs above the ground." These are a series of higher-level classical dressage movements in which all four feet of the horse actually leave the ground at one time (movements no longer used in competitive dressage). Andalusians are ancestors of the Lipizzan horse breed known worldwide for their beauty and grace in classical dressage. Andalusian colts are born dark, and their coat lightens through various shades of gray and eventually to white as they get older. I think Liponio was about eight or nine years old and was, by this time, almost completely white. He had a very, very long white mane that we braided in normal pigtail type braids to preserve it, and his full, white tail fell to the ground.

He did, however, unwittingly become another vivid illustration of God's sovereign protection over my life. I didn't have the time to saddle him up for a ride that day but wanted to be sure he at least got some exercise out of his box stall. So, I put a halter on him and led him out to the large arena to longe him. Longeing allows the horse to trot or canter in approximately a sixty-meter circle fastened to a longe-line or lead, much like an extra-long dog leash. Horses seem to enjoy the freedom, often bucking and carrying on freshly out of the stall, eventually settling down to a nice rhythmic trot or canter routine to the right and to the left.

I had worked Liponio to the right and, after I halted him, I was gathering up the line to prepare him to go to the left when suddenly something spooked him, and he bolted off in a dead run! The instant jerk caused the longe-line to fall out of my hands in one big clump to the ground. In shock and as if in slow motion, I looked down at the ground and saw the line unwinding as the horse got further and further away. Fearing Liponio would somehow escape the safety of the big arena, I quickly reached down and grabbed the line just as it was near the end. This particular line had a heavy rubber weight on the end of it, and the motion of grabbing and picking it up caused the rubber weight to swing a loop instantly around my wrist. With Liponio being at a gallop by this time, the line went taut, and I went flying into the air like a helium balloon, then flopped dead weight onto the ground on my belly with my left arm fully extended. I remember thinking, *I'm being dragged! Why can't I let go!?*

Still in seemingly slow motion, I looked up my arm and saw that my hand was trapped by the rubber piece. I looked beyond my hand, and all I could see was a vigorously swishing tail and hind hooves kicking up dust and dirt, heading for the opening in the arena. How was a one-ton animal going to be stopped by a ninety-pound weakling—namely me—tethered at the end of the line? My full weight on the line and being dragged along behind in the dirt didn't slow him a bit. He was like a greyhound pulling a toothpick! And there was no one else around, no one at all in sight.

I must have been dragged many yards before I even realized what was happening and what a serious predicament I was in! If Liponio made it to the opening in the fence, he would be in danger, and, worse yet, I would eventually be "roadkill!" Suddenly aware of real-time speed but without an inkling of what I could do about my situation, my mouth once again blurted out from the fear in my heart, "Lord, Jesus, save me!" reminiscent of run-away Fahrenheit. Instantly, Liponio turned in such a way that the longe-line slacked just a bit and gently wound around his back leg. In another nano-second, he stopped all on his own and turned around to face me. I watched in amazement (from my prone position) as the settling dust made it appear as though a blanket of peacefulness came over him, and he stood perfectly still and calm. I knew that God's peace on that horse was an immediate answer to my cry for help! I stood up, quickly untied my wrist from the line, brushed myself off, and tremblingly walked up to the horse. He was as calm as though nothing had happened. I took him back to his stall, telling no one of our harrowing brush with disaster. I was in shock from the unbelievable event that had just occurred. Even more unbelievable was the fact that I was walking back at all, too numb to feel sore.

However, by the next day, pain and limited movement in that arm forced me to get it examined. It turned out that I had sustained a severely strained ligament in my left upper arm. Careful use since then caused it to heal without surgery and full strength to be restored, but, every now and then, when I move it a certain way, I can feel a dull ache which reminds me of God's protection that day when my life was literally in danger. Who says pain isn't good?

God's absolute sovereignty over my life was made so vivid to me when I witnessed, once again, His complete control over the situation. He allowed it to happen, yet I could see His great and awesome power displayed over one of His creatures at a time when I was completely helpless. There was no bailing out for me this time. But God mercifully intervened on my behalf in a most remarkable way. He who *"rebuked the wind and the raging of the water, and they ceased and there was a calm"* on the Sea of Galilee (Luke 8:24, NKJV) also stilled beautiful Liponio, the storming animal of His creation. Again, a line from the hymn, "Be Still My Soul," reminded me, "The waves and wind *(and horses)* still know His voice who ruled them while He dwelt below."

Is there anything in life for which we cannot depend on Him? If He can stop a galloping horse that has a mind of its own, cannot He stop the wildest storms of our hearts that threaten to crash our very hopes and dreams on the rocky shores of life? The Gaither tune, "Because He Lives," reminds me: "I can face tomorrow." I can keep on keeping on. I can take one hope and one dream at a time and entrust them to Him, who is all-wise and knows what is best for me. *"O the depth of the riches both of the wisdom and knowledge of God; how unsearchable are His judgments and unfathomable His ways"* (Romans 11:33, KJV).

As time went on, God used sweet, obedient Liponio to stretch my confidence and ability even further as I learned how to properly handle and ride a stallion. Other than this unexpected incident on the ground, I actually reached a new plateau in my riding because, for the first time, I had the feeling that I was doing the riding rather than being taken for a ride. But, more importantly, the advancement in my spiritual pilgrimage was undeniable.

CHAPTER 5

A Magical World with Night Magic

"Some boast in chariots and some in horses,
But we will boast in the name
of the Lord our God."
(Psalm 20:7)

While I was becoming more familiar with stallions like Liponio, I became very aware that people everywhere just seem to love horses. Whether they're behind a fence along the road or on a street corner hooked up to a cart for a local vendor giving rides, they always seem to draw a crowd that wants to pet them or give them a treat. There's just something about them—their majesty, power, beauty. Of course, Frank and I were among those who stared in awe; and now we were close to them at the barn, touching them, petting them, giving them treats—Frank was a good sport to often join me in just hanging around or watching various exhibitions. Barbara had so many beauties—as I said earlier. Once I was finished riding Liponio, I loved going into the other horses' stalls, filling their water buckets, passing out carrots, and just about anything she would allow me to do.

Some of the greatest privileges I had was to be invited,

not only to watch all their horse shows but to be backstage, hands-on. There was tack to polish, manes and tails to brush, and big round bellies to shine. I never considered it work; for me, it was sheer fun. Sometimes there were roadshows where several riders and their mounts would travel to do an exhibition. They would ride together in military-like formation wearing flashy uniforms. I craved to ride with them, but I wasn't good enough yet. However, at one halftime entertainment in the infield of Santa Anita Racetrack, I was entrusted with supervising the loudspeaker music that accompanied their routine alongside the track staff. They were hired to be the entertainment in the infield during the major break between races. My heart pounded as I wanted to make sure everything came off without a hitch, which did much to the credit of the riders. The music was the easy part, but at least I was a part of the team. I liked that—a lot! To me, it was all magical.

There was one horse at the barn; however, that was the star of the show wherever he went. He was co-owned with Barbara, masterfully trained and ridden by Dianne Olds-Rossi, who rode him solo apart from the rest of the troop. His Dutch name was Arno, but his show name was "Night Magic," which was fitting for the awe he inspired. Was he ever that, and more.

He was a Friesian stallion imported from Europe. "Friesian horses originated in Friesland, a province of the Netherlands, (Holland)," according to the Internet.[1]

Although originally *bred* as a draft *horse*, the *breed* is graceful and nimble for its size and later developed into a finer-boned nobleman's steed. During the Middle Ages, *Friesian horses* were in great demand as destriers *(war horses)* throughout Europe since their size enabled them to carry a knight in full armor.[2]

I was told the stallions were distinguished in Holland as being carriage horses for the Queen. They were all black, and each one as majestic as the other. It was not often that Holland would export one of their stallions, but that was

1 fhana.com/the-friesian-horse/faq;
2 Internet: friesian-equine.co.uk/history-of-friesian-horse.html,

changing. Our majestic fellow was black too, big and beautiful. His mane was so full and long that it hung almost below
his knees. We had to braid it in big fat braids, put them into
long socks, fold those up and tie them at the top with ribbons
so that he would not step on them and pull his mane out!
Even his forelock was below the tip of his huge, long muzzle. That, too, had to be braided up out of his reach so that
he wouldn't accidently chew it off while eating. His tail was
almost overwhelming—at least two feet wide and very thick!
It could only be brushed in layers and had to be washed and
conditioned for shows. What a job! But what a privilege!

Dianne and Night Magic always drew a crowd. There
were always many exclamations of awe and approval and
much applause. Dianne's routine was called "High School"
(beyond the "schooling" of competitive dressage)—which
included some of the movements performed by the Spanish
Riding School of Vienna. Of course, they performed the
typical dressage movements of Piaffe, Passage, and Half-
pass. But she included the Spanish Walk where he lifted
each front leg up high and straight out, one step at a time; or
the Pedestal, where he would lift and tuck under one front
leg and turn his whole body around in a complete circle just
standing on the other front leg. During their canter, his long
flowing mane would practically wrap itself around Dianne
on his back. Dianne would make him rear or make him bow
at the end of their routine, which always brought thunderous
applause.

Dianne's most infamous costume was Darth Vader with
Night Magic covered in black and silver tack, looking like a

machine! She even had a glowing wand, and they performed in a darkened arena under a spotlight! It transformed all of us who watched with mouths open—up, up, and away to the famous Super Star Destroyer Flagship of the Jedi, which has been so popular.

A particularly unforgettable trip was when Barbara and Dianne asked me to accompany them to a famous rodeo coliseum in Texas, where Dianne was hired to do an exhibition representing *The Magical World of Dancing Horses*. Her legendary Hollywood stuntman, trick-riding, cowboy husband, Rex Rossi, was also a featured entertainer for the event. Frank encouraged me to go over the weekend while he held down the fort at home. The twelve-hour trip there was unforgettable, as I was given a turn at the wheel of the truck hauling two-million-dollar stallions in the back while the rest of the crew slept! Gratefully, having never hauled before, I was able to give them some rest and keep the truck on the road! We were met by a whole crew of police escorts and coliseum staff which joined our group assisting Dianne and Arno.

Barbara and Rex on the left in black jackets;
Diane and Arno Center, me on the right

Once there, my first job was to be a rope handler for Rex. In the middle of the arena, with up-tempo Western music blaring, he would sit or stand in the Western saddle of his beautiful Quarter Horse and perform roping tricks all around and over his very obedient steed that didn't move a muscle. Then he would throw the rope down, jump off the horse and do the "Texas Skip" through a huge loop from a different rope. The loop was vertical this time and at least five feet high in diameter. Rex would jump through the sideways loop from one side to the other without missing a "skip." He was great fun to watch, and the audience loved him. I enjoyed being out there with him, just following him around and picking up the ropes he discarded.

Rex had been quite famous in the Hollywood scene, doing stunts for cowboy actors in the popular Western shows of the time. When we were at home base, I could always spot Rex on the trail even if it was a half-mile away—he had a way of sitting on his horse that was poetic, pure Rex Rossi, as though they were born together with him in the saddle.

Meanwhile, my daily function at the Texas show was to groom Arno after each of Dianne's rides, sponging off the sweat, and lovingly brushing his big muscular body and abundant hair. People gathered around the portable stall the coliseum had set up for him. They had just seen him perform as Night Magic and wanted to admire him up close. He made me feel like a celebrity as people were envious that I was able to spend such quality time with him. I ate it up—the closest to fleeting fame I would ever get for rubbing shoulders with a famous trainer/equestrian and her majestic *Night Magic!*

We were there for two days, with two shows a day, and Arno and I became quite attached. In fact, Barbara told me that he would nicker when he saw me approaching. That made my heart swell.

The trip home was tiring but thankfully uneventful in the negative sense of the term, and we were all glad to put the horses in their own stalls and head for our own beds. The next morning, I arose in anticipation of seeing my new buddy again and giving him carrots as I had been doing in Texas. There he was, hanging his beautiful massive head out of his stall door, and I joyfully opened it up and walked in, closing the door behind me, ready to hug his big neck.

All of a sudden, he attacked! He lunged at me with mouth wide and bared teeth glistening! I screamed and backed into the corner but was hampered by the corner feed bucket. I was trapped, and if he came at me again, I would be in real danger. It all happened so fast, and I was in shock. Barbara had heard my scream and came running, shooing him away from me, and got me out to safety. *What happened?* My mind raced. *Why was he turning on me?* I was frightened, trembling, and heartbroken. The only thing we could ascertain was that being a stallion, his stall was *his* territory, and I had not established myself within that parameter before the show so that after the show, I was suddenly an intruder. Who knew? I never went in there again and was always cautious around his stall after that. But he still loved being groomed outside his stall for local shows, and I pampered him every chance I got.

With the power displayed by Arno's mass of muscle, I could understand for the first time why in ancient days, the horse was used as a war machine. In fact, Scripture describes that sad history of this beautiful creation of God:

> *Do you give the horse his might? Do you clothe his neck with a mane? Do you make him leap like the locust? His majestic snorting is terrible. (English Standard Version aptly reads "terrifying.") He paws in the valley, and rejoices in his strength; he goes out to meet the weapons. He laughs at fear and is not dismayed; and he does not turn back*

from the sword. The quiver rattles against him, the flashing spear and javelin. With shaking and rage he races over the ground, and he does not stand still at the voice of the trumpet. As often as the trumpet sounds he says, "Aha!" and he scents the battle from afar, and the thunder of the captains and the war cry (Job 39:19-25).

Also, in Revelation 19:11, a beautiful horse will be ridden by our victorious King Jesus Christ, who returns for the final battle against those who hate God, to set up His righteous kingdom on earth for those of us who believe in Him. As Proverbs 21:31 says: *"The horse is made ready for the day of battle, but the victory belongs to the Lord"* (ESV).

I, for one, would not want to be on the receiving end of the Lord's wrath, nor that of His warhorse! Thank God the Scripture also teaches in Isaiah 11:6 that the day will come, soon, when the Lord returns, and war is taught no more:

The wolf will dwell with the lamb, and the leopard will lie down with the young goat, and the calf and the young lion and the fatling together; and a little boy will lead them.

However, I think it's awesome that, of all of God's beautifully created animals, the horse is *the one* animal that Jesus has chosen for the privilege of carrying Him back to earth in victory—this magnificent creature carrying his majestic Creator on his back! According to Revelation 19:11-16:

And I saw heaven opened, and behold, a white horse, and He who sat on it is called Faithful and True, and in righteousness He judges and wages war. His eyes are a flame of fire, and on His head are many diadems; and He has a name written on Him which no one knows except Himself. He is clothed with a robe dipped in blood, and His name is called The Word of God. And the armies which are in heaven, clothed in fine linen, white and clean, were following Him on white horses. From His mouth comes a sharp sword, so that with it He may strike down the nations, and He will rule them with a rod of iron; and He treads the wine press of the fierce wrath of God, the Almighty. And on His robe and on His thigh He has a name written, "KING OF KINGS, AND LORD OF LORDS."

CHAPTER 6

From Modern Creation

To Masquerade

"And He will bring forth your righteousness as
the light,
And your judgment as the noonday.
Rest in the Lord, and wait patiently for Him. "
(Psalm 37:6-7)

It was around this time when the '94 Northridge 6.7 magnitude earthquake hit the Los Angeles area. Our Canyon Country house on the other side of that mountain range was heavily damaged, especially at the foundation, so we were advised to move. The main floor literally had to be gutted in order to install rebar to reinforce the foundation. Again, it was Barbara to the rescue as she had friends in Burbank renting a condo from her that was a three-bedroom. She offered, and they graciously agreed to let us move in as roommates until the repairs could be accomplished. They became dear friends. The condo was right outside LAEC, along the trail path that I had often ridden, so it was thrilling to be able to go out on the front veranda and watch riders passing by or horses being schooled in the arenas over the wall. It was a special time for both Frank and me to enjoy.

Then Liponio was moved out of the barn, so I was put on the back of a gorgeous American Saddlebred stallion named Modern Creation, owned, of course, by Barbara. He was a real head-turner—a tri-color pinto: brown, white and black. He had a black-and-white mane and tail with lots of white on his shoulders and rump that ran down his legs like a spilled can of white paint. He was gorgeous. Barbara even arranged a photoshoot for us which was another unexpected thrill for me as I donned her Saddle Seat show clothes which fit me perfectly.

As a Saddlebred, Modern had been trained to pull a cart and was national champion in the sport of driving. In the world of sport driving, the horse would be hitched to a wagon, carriage, cart, or sleigh by means of a harness. Modern was fun to watch pulling a two-wheeled cart manned by his driver. By the time I got him, he was still a healthy and sound twenty-two-year-old, retired from the show scene but being used for breeding. And he made beautiful babies! He was such a nice horse—having a friendly and kind demeanor.

Modern became my first attempt at actually *training* a horse instead of just honing my personal equestrian skills. I began to practice the dressage I had learned on Fefe and had resumed with Liponio. How gratifying it was to have Modern respond to me and begin to pick up the precise movements of that discipline. But there was one problem. Age had taken its toll on him, and he had a sway back which caused me to sit incorrectly in the saddle. Proper dressage is accomplished much by the way one sits, and I was becoming frustrated with being unable to practice my equitation properly. I wanted to compete as I had done with Fefe. Plus, the relentless practicing and training can be difficult on a horse—it's like working out at the gym—and I didn't really want to put Modern through it. He had paid his dues. Since he had already been trained to drive, I felt it was time for him to enjoy his retirement and not work so hard to learn something new. So Modern and I just enjoyed being out together.

We were even on the six o'clock evening news in Los Angeles as a backdrop to the weather report because his beauty drew such attention. Riding the perimeter of the park, being in the sunshine, enjoying a good trot or canter was great fun. Riding him was like sitting in a rocking chair.

However, I began to pray about someday having a good dressage horse of my very own. Unknown to me at the time, God was using Modern to instill in me the confidence I would need for my future efforts in training instead of just being trained. When I realized that later, I was reminded about the fact that the Lord wastes nothing in our lives: *"There is an appointed time for everything. And there is a time for every event under heaven"* (Ecclesiastes 3:1). When one tracks their experiences in life, one can see how they all begin to fit together like a puzzle, and something that didn't make sense at one point will often have an explanation or be put to good use later on.

I had been riding Modern for a year when Barbara told me that I could ride the stallion's colt, *Masquerade* (nicknamed *"Mack"*), whose mare was pure Hanoverian (German bred—perfect for dressage). Barbara always made sure I had a horse to ride! The colt was a striking three-year-old with markings similar to his sire and was just being saddle-broke. I was so looking forward to riding Mack when he was ready that I would visit his stall every day just to admire him. Once again, Barbara set up a photoshoot and allowed me the privilege of holding his reins off-camera since he was not saddle broke yet. It was literally the first time he and I "met" outside his stall and interacted.

Shortly thereafter, I learned that there was another girl who also wanted to ride the horse, and she seemed just as excited about riding him as I was. Rather than allow a problem to develop between our schedules, I told Barbara that I believed the right thing to do was to let her ride Mack, even though I felt very sad and disappointed. Privately through tears, I brought my disappointment to God in prayer. I was reminded of how kind and gracious He had always been to me, and I was confident that if He wanted me to ride the horse, He would bring it to pass; if not, I was trusting in His perfect will. I rode Modern for another year and put Mack completely out of my mind. He was even moved to another barn, and I didn't expect to ever see him again.

Eventually, Frank and I began to discuss and pray about the possibility of purchasing a horse of my own. Through the years, he had made some wise decisions and built up a bit of savings. In *another* gesture of generosity, he was willing to give me $5,000 to find a nice competition horse.

And he was willing to make a financial commitment for the care and training it would take even beyond the purchase of the animal we chose. But it would be a big sacrifice. Other household items would have to stay on "hold."

A Perfect Match

During the following summer, I talked to Barbara again and asked if she knew of a good dressage horse that might be for sale. She said that Mack (I hadn't heard that name for a year and a half!) hadn't worked out for the other girl she had allowed to ride him and that he was for sale—but she wanted $15,000 for him (the price put him completely out of the picture). Nevertheless, she suggested I go to his stable and ride him just to see how I liked him under saddle. The odd thing was that the minute I heard Mack's name, I didn't even want to look at another horse. I didn't want to shop around. In my heart, I wanted him to be the one, but we couldn't afford him. Then Barbara made an astounding statement: she might consider letting me have him for $7,000 if I liked him (which was so much closer to our limit)! Amazing!

I went to see Mack, who was being stabled at Keenridge, Hilda Gurney's farm in Moorpark. I had been there several times with Barbara and was looking forward to seeing Hilda again along with the colt. Sure enough, there he was, and it was love at first (second) sight.

He greeted me warmly as I stretched out my hand, his soft muzzle obviously searching for a treat. He had kind, attentive eyes and seemed glad to have a visitor. His coat was clean and smooth, smelling of the warmth of the day. I would always take a deep breath when I arrived at any stable, loving the mixture of aromas: the indescribable essence of equine, various hays, straws, or bedding on the ground, and, of course, manure. In fact, one day, while at work, I went to lunch with some of the girls from the office. We rounded the corner from the parking lot approaching the front of the restaurant when the aroma of freshly laid fertilizer for the grass assaulted their nostrils. "Phewww" was their response. Mine was, "Ahhh, manure."

The "Ahhh" I was now experiencing was more than that - it was the joy of being in the presence of this beautiful animal I thought I had lost. He was just as gorgeous as I remembered him—like his father. Hilda's assistant pulled Mack out of his stall for me, and we put him in the cross-ties. He was still a baby at four and a half years old (a horse's mind doesn't really mature until at least nine years old), but he was more settled than when I first met him as a three-year-old. He stood quietly while we saddled him, and I felt a bit nervous when we got to Hilda's dressage arena, I think mostly because I so terribly wanted this reunion to work out. What if he and I didn't hit it off well under saddle? But we proceeded nicely and, as I rode him for the first time in front of Hilda, she said we seemed to be a perfect match. Needless to say, I trusted her judgment! She said Mack had a tender mouth, and it was important for his rider to have soft hands (that meant not always clinging to or tugging on the reins which were attached to the bit inside the horse's soft mouth). Otherwise, as time goes by, the horse can become hard in the mouth and less responsive to the rider's aids. She had even given him an especially gentle bit. Thankfully, Hilda said I had "good hands." I excitedly called Barbara and told her of my compatible experience on Mack's back according to Hilda's expert opinion, and I expressed my interest in taking the horse. She wisely suggested I have a veterinarian examine him to make sure he was healthy and sound.

The following week when the vet examined him, to my dismay, Mack's left front foot was slightly sore, and he had a mild temperature. He appeared to be in top condition in every other way, but the vet wouldn't sign the release papers for the sale. She said that the sore foot could be fine in a week or two, but it might also be an ongoing weakness. She suggested that I ride the horse for a few weeks to see if the condition would clear up.

Since Mack's stable was an hour's drive from Burbank, where we lived, I made a request to Barbara: could I move the horse to my condo area where he would be closer to me? A free stall was made available to each renter, so I wouldn't have to pay board (and it would relieve her of the daily expense she was already incurring). That way, I could ride him often to see if he became sound, and I'd be able to make a decision on whether to buy him. She not only agreed but also offered a lower sale price of $5,000 if he became sound—the very amount Frank and I had decided was my limit! My heart leapt at the thought!

On a bright, sunny day in August, I borrowed Barbara's truck and trailer and went to Moorpark and loaded up Mack. What an exciting, first-time experience that was for me as I contemplated having the sole responsibility for this huge, dependent animal. I felt like a new mother! The day before, when I was preparing the bedding in his new stall and hanging saddle and bridle racks in his new tack room, I

had the overwhelming sense of what it must be like to prepare a nursery for the arrival of a new baby (having never
had one of my own). And my baby was 1,200 pounds! I
hauled him home, and he took up residence in his new stall.
He was so close to our condo that I could look out and see
him from our kitchen window and even hear him whinny.
Be still my heart!

I began to ride him the very next morning. After a couple of weeks, I told Barbara that I thought he was sound,
and his lameness was only temporary. At that point, she
made another astounding statement: "You know, Pat, I really don't care about the money. You can have the horse."
Not believing what I had just heard, I declined the offer
and told her that I wanted to *own* the horse outright, not
just ride him as I had done with her other horses. After she
insisted and reassured me that she wanted me to *have* the
horse, I accepted! Mack became my very own—another
direct answer to my specific prayer! God again faithfully
worked on my behalf through my kind friend's generosity.

There was a spiritual principle in operation on the day I
was willing to give Mack up a year and a half earlier while
trusting in God's perfect will for me. God reminded me of
what I had learned when He first gave me Annie to ride,
that whatever I am willing to give up for His sake, He often
returns as an unexpected reward in some way. God might
even repay a hundred-fold according to Mark 10:29-30:

Jesus said, "Truly I say to you, there is no one who has left house or brothers or sisters or mother or father or children or farms, for My sake and for the gospel's sake, but that he shall receive a hundred times as much now in the present age, houses and brothers and sisters and mothers and children and farms, along with persecutions; and in the age to come, eternal life."

Anything we surrender for His glory, for His sake, He will bless. Some way, somehow, someday we will see the goodness of the Lord if we just wait and trust. Now He was giving me my very own horse—and *the very* horse that was the apple of my eye! His goodness is immeasurable! As the Bible says, *"Every good thing given and every perfect gift is from above, coming down from the Father of lights..."* (James 1:17a).

There is another little, but not insignificant, detail about how the Lord pays attention to the desires of our hearts. As I'd ridden the various horses over the past decade, I often thought about what color I would want my horse to be. I decided long before that I liked either the bay (a brown horse with a black mane and tail) or the pinto. As it turned out, Mack's parents were both: the sire, Modern Creation, passed along the pinto coloring, and the dam was a bay. So along came Mack with his gorgeous tri-color pinto markings but also with the markings typical of a bay, especially on his head. For example, his overall color was chestnut (kind of a copper-penny color). But he had black around his eyes, black outlining his ears and his muzzle, along with a black tail and black and white mane. Also, a bay horse often has four black knee socks, but Mack had four evenly matched, white knee-socks and white on his shoulders, neck, and muzzle that resembled his beautiful father. Quite a combination! To add to my delight, he had the profile of a lamb's head on his forehead, which was a constant reminder to me that he was a gift from the "Lamb of God," my Lord and Savior Jesus Christ. He looked to me like the Lord's masterpiece with a paintbrush! Hilda said he had "presence."

I believe that the Lord provided my very own horse, with all the attention he would need and the responsibility it placed on me alone, as a marvelous diversion at that specific time in my life. During the previous year and a half, in addition to the deaths of my parents, my wonderful schoolmaster, Fefe, and other pets, with the Northridge earthquake displacing us from our home for nearly two years, it was a time of emotional ups and downs. Although thankful for the other mounts I had been riding and enjoying, receiving my wonderful horse helped to keep me from focusing on difficult circumstances and reminded me that, along with the bitter things of life, God grants us blessings to brighten us. He shows us that He is always near to care for us and to teach us to wait upon Him—never giving up hope: *"Casting all your anxiety on Him because He cares for you"* (1 Peter 5:7).

Mikwaiti, "My Hope"

Wanting to acknowledge God's hand in giving me Mack and realizing the perfect timing of His gift, I decided to give Mack a new name. The Lord had taught me to "wait" upon His perfect timing. Since the horse was a token of His perfect love toward me and a response to my trust in Him—I called the horse "Mik-*wait*-i." "Mikwaiti" was, in fact, very close in pronunciation to the Greek word, *"miqweh"* found in the Brown-Driver-Briggs Hebrew and English Lexicon used in various verses to describe "something waited for, i.e., Confidence—hope." When we wait in faith upon the Lord, trusting in His goodness toward us, we are filled with hope, which is an expectation of seeing that goodness manifested on our behalf. "Mikwaiti" became his show name; however, since the wait was over, and my hope was fulfilled, I removed the "*wait*" in his name and called his barn name "Miki." So Mikwaiti was another demonstration of God's goodness in my life, giving me hope for a better future. He also connected me with Miki's past quite unexpectedly.

Desperado

On one of my vacation days, a weekday when hardly anyone else was around, I took Miki over to the practice arena at the Equestrian Center next door to the condo. While we were practicing the different gaits and movements, another rider entered the arena. I was very aware of her gazing at us. I asked her if I was in her way (maybe she was supposed to take a lesson, and I wasn't supposed to be in the ring?). She told me no, so we kept on riding.

Finally, she asked with a German accent, "Is that Desperado?"

"No," I replied, "this is Mikwaiti, formerly known as Masquerade, but I just changed his name."

"I knew it!" she exclaimed. She told me her name was Jutta. "Masquerade used to be called Desperado," she continued. "I'd know those markings anywhere! He was born to my mare, and that's what I named him. I had him for several months and fully intended to keep him because he was such a beautiful baby. I even took pictures of him back with me to Germany when I went to visit my mother. My German friends were so taken with his markings that they were offering me $15,000 for him just from the baby pictures! But I wouldn't sell. Unfortunately, I later had some financial difficulties and had to let him go quickly." She, of course, had sold the colt to Barbara, the owner of his sire, Modern Creation (Jutta had previously purchased Modern's semen from Barbara to impregnate her Hanoverian mare). Here he was, now four and a half years old, and she hadn't seen him since he was six months.

Jutta was happy to see him again and glad to know that he was owned by somebody who loved him. I was excited to meet her because I had a million questions, like:

"When was he born?" *(May 23, 1991)*

"Do you still have any baby pictures?" (*Yes*)

"Could I have copies?" *(Of course!)*

"What was his mother like?" *(A great breeding mare named Soubrette, who is from a good Hanoverian line of jumpers).*

Did she have pictures of the mare? *(Yes—and you can have those too!)*

It was a wonderful time of getting filled in on Miki's past. As I sorted through all of the pictures Jutta gave me, I could see exactly how she was able to recognize the colt. His markings were so unique, no matter what size he was. One always wonders about a horse's past and wishes they could speak to tell you if they had been traumatized in any way, what their health issues were, why they had their particular idiosyncrasies, etc. Fortunately, Miki was raised in a healthy environment by people who loved him, and he had not gone through many hands before coming to me. His mind didn't seem to be messed up from any unknown trauma. These were important details.

I marveled at the timing of all of that: my having a day off, just happening to ride in that particular arena at that unusual time of the morning with no one else around except the two riders who discovered their unexpected connection.

Amazing. Once again, God was providing details for me that answered questions in my heart that hadn't even been uttered. The Bible says in Psalm 139:4, *"Even before there is a word on my tongue, behold O Lord, You know it all."* And again, in Matthew 6:8, *"...for your Father knows what you need, before you ask Him."* What joy! What comfort! What a great, generous, loving God we have!

Little did I know that in God's kind providence, Miki would be reunited four years later with this very special someone from his past whom, I discovered—and had not known at the time of our first meeting—was a German Certified Trainer—Jutta Heinsohn! Much later on, we received some wonderful training from her, and she enjoyed the contact with "Desperado" again at her ranch. Having personally trained dressage in Germany, she was able to use her expertise to help other riders like me and my friend who accompanied me to her facility. I enjoyed letting Jutta see Miki's movements. She worked with us on riding the diagonal, learning to enhance the impulsion without increasing speed. The challenge was in pushing Miki forward and letting his frame powerfully stretch out longer but without the temptation to hold him back in the bridle. I wondered how Jutta felt watching us ride and wondered if she regretted having had to sell him. I'm sure she did early on when he was a yearling, but we never discussed it further. In my mind, who would *not* regret letting Miki go to someone else? But that was probably just me.

CHAPTER 7

Training, Training, Training: What's the Point?

*"All discipline for the moment seems not
to be joyful, but sorrowful;
Yet to those who have been trained
by it, Afterwards it yields the peaceful
fruit of righteousness."*
(Hebrews 12:11)

Being a horse *owner* rather than a *borrower* carried
many responsibilities, many of them financial. Each time
the Lord provided what I needed, we were astounded over
and over again. For instance, I began to look for serious
training for Miki and me. He was still a baby at four and
a half years old (the "terrible twos") and was a handful,
to say the least, especially in comparison to the seasoned
horses I had known. I had never attempted to handle a
young horse before (all 1,100 pounds of him) and found
myself at a loss as to the baby equine thought processes
and behaviors. In fact, after Miki began to acclimate to
his new surroundings, he was being bothered by sensory
overload. His attitude seemed to deteriorate into downright
disobedience (from my unlearned perspective). In reality, I

eventually learned I had not yet won his respect and trust as a "lead" animal. I couldn't get him to even walk around the park trail without having a major battle on my hands if he saw something that scared him. He intimidated me with his strength and strong will. All he wanted to do was turn and run—the "fright and flight mechanism" that keeps horses alive in the wild. He would whirl, plant his feet, or go backward. He would half-rear, or he would just plain stand still and refuse to go forward. My previous experiences had not covered these scenarios. I needed help—and fast—so I called in the "cavalry."

Ride 'em Cowboy

His name was Alan Hicks. He was an ex-rodeo rider and had the reputation of being able to ride anything! It was the entertainment of the day to watch Alan at work. He could mount a horse that was so big a person couldn't even reach the stirrup from the ground—and he would run to it with an effortless leap, planting his pointed cowboy boot precisely where it needed to be in the left/near stirrup that was chest high, and gracefully swinging his other leg over the saddle before the horse knew what was happening. Someone was always telling a story about what they had seen Alan accomplish in and out of the ring. But Alan didn't come for free, and yet somehow the money was there. So, I hired him for a month. He wanted thirty days to get my colt into ride-able shape for me so that he would be something I could handle out on the trail. Alan explained that Miki needed to be worked longer hours than I had been able to do up to that point in order to get his youthful energy all out of his system, to come back to his stall tired and content; that he was a healthy, energetic horse that would continually put me to the test to determine who the "alpha" was—him or me. That's the way it is in a herd. One mare becomes dominant over all the other mares and their babies, even young colts. Eventually, the dominant stallion decides it's time for a maturing colt to leave his mare's herd and go off to build a different herd of mares for himself. Well, this "mare" (*me*) had a lot to learn.

Alan used his western saddle on Miki for a more secure seat and his favorite "baby bit" (a Western Pelham) that would make him pay closer attention. It made me think of the Scripture that says:

> *Do not be as the horse or as the mule which have no understanding, whose trappings include bit and bridle to hold them in check, otherwise they will not come near to you. Many are the sorrows of the wicked; but he who trusts in the Lord, lovingkindness shall surround him* (Psalm 32:9-10).

How often had I been obstinate with the Lord to the point that He had to yank on *my* "bit"? How many times had I kicked up my heels against the Lord and refused to listen in order to go my own way? If I would only trust Him completely, fear would be gone, and loving-kindness would surround me! Miki gave me very visual lessons. I often drew these kinds of parallels between Miki and me and then with the Lord and me. It was a daily lesson that made me want to be more sensitive to the leading of our patient, heavenly Father who loves us and is able to keep us safe: *"Now unto Him who is able to keep you from falling, and to present you faultless before the presence of His glory with exceeding joy"* (Jude 1:24, KJV).

Alan began to ride Miki through the Hollywood hills every day while I went to work. When I came home, there was my sweet boy so tired that all he wanted to do was lay down in his stall and sleep! Alan reported what a good horse he was—willing and strong. He just needed to know who was boss and that his "boss" could be trusted. So that's where my training came in… to learn to be the boss.

One weekend, Alan finally took us both out at the same time, but he rode Miki while I rode Alan's well-trained mare. We went out on the winding trails of Griffith Park overlooking Hollywood on a beautiful, sunny Saturday morning, and I watched in awe as he put Miki through his paces from the very beginning, making him go precisely where Alan wanted him to go, not where the horse preferred to go; I couldn't help but admire how beautiful Miki looked under saddle being ridden by someone else since he was usually under me! Alan never mistreated him but was consistent and firm.

Alan challenged me to keep up with them if I could and

took off at a gallop. Not to be outdone, much less left alone in the Hollywood hills, and on Alan's trustworthy steed, I took off close behind. We rode up and down, around and through. We took deer trails, and footpaths and fire roads. Alan would turn around in the saddle and look back to see if he had left us in the dust—but he hadn't. We were right there at his heels! Finally, we slowed down to a walk to give the horses a rest and began our "trail chat." I was able to share with Alan why I had changed Miki's name from Masquerade to Mikwaiti and was glad for the opportunity to speak a word for the Lord. Soon, I asked Alan about a very steep incline called Suicide Hill that I had heard about. Had he ever been on it?

"Sure," he said, "many times!" In fact, he knew those mountains so well; many of the trails we followed were old deer paths he had enhanced through the years. I marveled once again at how docile and obedient Miki was with him as we all sauntered along together on loose reins. He was too tired to think about a fight and fully respected the man on his back! I chuckled at the thought.

We swayed along swapping horse stories when Alan instructed me to follow him along a deer path single file. We wound around a few seemingly unmarked trails and began to descend over a ridge. Alan instructed, "Just lean back in the saddle and let your legs go out straight in front of you. Give the horse her head by loosening the reins but keep her nose straight, and follow me." By that time, I was as obedient as Miki—doing exactly what the master rider said.

As the mare began to follow Alan and Miki down, I found myself really leaning back and almost standing in my stirrups that were practically parallel to the horse's shoulders, literally lying on the mare's back. I envisioned that if the horse disappeared from underneath me, I would be standing on the level ground below. I looked down and saw Alan, totally undaunted, turning around on Miki's back and looking up at us.

"Are you okay?" he asked.

"Yep, we're fine!" I answered. I watched Miki slide down partway, almost sitting on his rump in front of us but keeping his balance quite well. The mare was doing the same.

Finally, at the bottom, we found level ground, and I caught up to Alan and Miki, and we resumed riding side by side.

"So, were you scared?" Alan asked.

"Naw, that wasn't too bad," I honestly replied.

"Well, congratulations; you just went down Suicide Hill!" He laughed as my face went purple. Had I known ahead of time, my fear would have prevented me from going, I'm sure. But Alan treated me no differently than he treated his horses. He oozed such confidence that our trust in him could make us do things we never thought we could do. That was the kind of trust I needed to instill in Miki toward me. And that is the kind of trust God, *"the Lord of hosts,"* wants us to have in Him, *"who tries the feelings* (lit. the reins) *of the heart"* (Jeremiah 11:20).

By the time we got back to the stall, two hours had gone by. Alan turned Miki back over to me and paid me one of the highest compliments I could have ever heard from a true-grit cowboy like him. He said I road as well as he did that day!

The following weekend we went out together again, but this time Alan had me on Miki's back through the hills. We were doing fine until we came to a slight foot-wide precipice that Miki refused to cross over. This was a typical example of how Miki would get the upper hand with me. He just wouldn't do it, and I didn't know how to make him. From there, the whole "who's boss" idea would deteriorate. Miki would refuse on one thing, then another, then silly things—just at his whim. I had to establish that I was the dominant animal if this horse was going to trust me and obey me. I thought of the old hymn verse, "Trust and obey, for there's no other way, to be happy in Jesus, but to trust and obey." The scriptural application of my relationship with the Lord came booming into my mind often: *"...you are each one walking according to the stubbornness of his own evil heart, without listening to Me"* (Jeremiah 16:12). I never wanted that! I often examined my heart to make sure it was right before the Lord. I always wanted to please my heavenly Master-Teacher!

Alan's confident tone assured me, "Just do exactly as I tell you. If he turns away to the right, you hold onto your left rein and nudge him hard with your right leg. If he turns to the left, hold steady your right rein and nudge him with your left leg. Don't give him anywhere to go but straight. Got it?"

"Oh sure," I gulped. So, we started forward to give it a try. Miki went left; Alan shouted, "Right rein, right rein, left leg!" Miki went right; Alan yelled, "Left rein, right leg!" Over and over again, I followed his every word until, finally, Miki went over the precipice! Wow! I had won!

"Not so fast," Alan said. "Do it again. Bring him back this way." I started back. "Right, left, no, no, left, no, yes, right," he would yell. Finally, Miki listened to me as I listened to Alan, and back across the small precipice, we came. "Do it again!" We did, again and again. Finally, Miki was just walking over. After that experience, I stopped having that kind of stubborn refusal with him. Anywhere we went, he knew he must obey me because he could trust that I would never take him anywhere that would hurt him. But the best part of it was I knew I was boss, and if he didn't want to obey, I now knew what to do.

After that, we didn't need Alan too much anymore. We were more or less through the worst of it. There was a day, however, while I was riding the three-mile perimeter of the

Equestrian Center when Miki saw men in a utility truck way up ahead that were working on a telephone pole, and he refused to take another step. I could have demanded as Alan had taught me, but another thing I learned was that it's wise to pick your battles. Alan told me there are some places where it's not safe to tangle with a horse—like on the side of a hill or next to a cliff, or where we were. We happened to be at the entrance to LAEC, where there was asphalt and periodic cars driving through. So, for that day, I decided it was best not to force the issue, but I knew allowing his fear of the utility truck would escalate into something else in the future. It wasn't just a matter of waiting a number of days for the truck to move. Once Miki got it in his head that he had "won" the battle of wills at that spot, there would be no getting him past it—at least not for me. So, it was Alan to the rescue again.

We made arrangements to meet there the next day. Alan drove up right where Miki and I stood next to the curb, replaced my English saddle and bridle with his own Western tack, hopped on Miki, and started to ask him to cross the asphalt. Nope, Miki didn't want to budge even with Alan on his back. Left and right, they zigged and zagged, but there was no going forward—at least not easily. Alan made progress with a few forward steps across the asphalt. As he asked Miki to step up the curb on the other side onto the dirt footing, Miki attempted to evade again by sidestepping. Suddenly, his hind feet gave out underneath him on the asphalt, and he slipped down on his side. It was like poetry in motion because Alan just pulled his leg away from under the horse as he was going down but kept the outside leg still in the stirrup. When Miki rolled onto his side and then began to roll right back up again, Alan was still there, still on his back, still in the saddle. Miki looked shocked. He just couldn't get rid of this guy! It was then that Miki relented and began to go obediently forward. He was still afraid, but he respected Alan more than his fear of the utility truck, and they began to trot past it, which had been about fifty yards ahead. Pretty soon, Alan had Miki cantering up past the truck and back again, over and over.

Of course, the success had to be owned by me as well. Watching Alan and Miki go by the truck was one thing, but my getting Miki to do it as well was another. So, Alan had me get on Miki's back. He stood and watched, yelling instructions as we came nearer to the truck. Miki's ears were perked and his eyes wide with his canter a little swift, but he was obedient to my cues. We rode another fifty yards past the truck, turned around, and came back. Alan had us do that several times until he was confident we wouldn't have any more trouble as Miki got over his fear.

I kept thinking about fear and how it paralyzes us from moving forward, from accomplishing simple tasks. The right kind of fear; *"The fear of the Lord,"* says the Scripture *"is the beginning of knowledge; Fools despise wisdom and instruction"* (Proverbs 1:7), and *"The fear of the Lord is the beginning of wisdom; A good understanding have all those who do His commandments"* (Psalm 111:10). So, obedience to God's Word is evidence of that awesome reverence in our hearts for God. I would often marvel at the spiritual principles that would flood my mind while dealing with Miki's baby-horse antics. Jesus used several illustrations of man's understanding of sheep to explain His teachings. For instance, the Bible says in the gospel of John, *"I am the good shepherd, and I know My own and My own know Me"* (John 10:14). When we know Jesus, we trust Him and follow Him in obedience, like sheep following their shepherd. In similar fashion, the Holy Spirit used my relationship with Miki to show me the value of fearing God and not circumstances, trusting that wherever He would lead me would always be for my good.

Training with a Purpose

Finally, the time came for Frank and me to be able to move back to our newly renovated home in Santa Clarita, nearly a thirty-mile drive. That meant losing the free stall that came with the condo we had lived in for eighteen months. Since Miki was all mine and not a borrowed horse from Barbara, his expenses were all mine as well. In an effort to keep costs lower, I moved Miki to a friend's home with boarding in Burbank, not far from the Equestrian Center. She had a couple of stalls in her backyard, and I was grateful for the opportunity. Her name was Phyllis, and we enjoyed our friendship and riding together there. It was nice, right near the trails, but then I had the problem of not being connected to a dressage trainer or arena. All the things I had been given through the years as a gift were now my responsibility, and it was expensive. Once again, I thanked God for how wonderfully generous Barbara had been to me through the years. But *Lord, now what?* I moaned.

One morning, Miki and I were out in the field called Pollywog behind Phyllis' house, where I longed him in our makeshift arena made up of a couple of large circles worn into the dirt and grass.

A rider came around the corner of the trail. He had a beautiful horse that was obviously well trained, and the man's equitation was admirable. We chatted about each other's horses, and, lo and behold; I discovered that he was a trainer named Bud Muravez. Bud's own barn was just the other side of the Equestrian Center, not far from Phyllis' place. I asked if I could come and observe a lesson which he gladly accommodated. So, I drove over one Saturday morning and liked what I saw. Bud was older, experienced, an upper-level competitive dressage rider himself who was known for competing in sunglasses! He was a kind but demanding instructor. As I watched the lesson, I could tell he knew his stuff. His price was reasonable—cheaper than what I would have had to pay at the Eq. Center. I could easily ride-walk Miki there, so we began to take lessons once a week. Naturally, when a good trainer is discovered, word spreads, and before we knew it, Bud had a small group of "disciples" with my friends and me.

We trained with Bud for about three months. He really liked Miki—said he had "pizzazz" and "chrome" because of his unusual markings and was excited about Miki's potential, and that he was flashy enough to draw the attention of the judges in the show arena. It was beautiful to watch Bud riding Miki once in a while. I could see from a distance how good he looked when an experienced dressage rider put him into the conformational "frame" required for the sport. We all were growing under Bud's tutelage—that is—until Easter of that year.

It was right at that time that I had decided to write a small pocket-sized booklet about Miki entitled *Mikwaiti "My Hope"* (the predecessor to this written work) which was the story in previous chapters of how I had gotten Miki and why I changed his name. Those kinds of details were always interesting to horse people. It was nearly impossible to meet someone on the trail, exchange greetings, admire each other's horses, and then ride off without telling how each one acquired their equine partner. That's just the way it was done. I decided rather than tell the long, wonderful story over and over again, I would write it down and simply hand it out. I wanted to give God the glory for it all, so I added some paragraphs about finding salvation through Jesus Christ. It was my feeble attempt at honoring God by giving Him public thanks and praise for His love and generosity to me. I had decided to have the booklet ready by Easter.

That's when we got the news about Bud. He came out

for his regular training session with us but notified us that he had been diagnosed with cancer. He was visibly shaken, and we were shocked! I took my brand-new booklet out of my purse and handed a copy to Bud. I told him it was a Christian testimony, and he seemed grateful to take it. He said he would read it with his wife on Easter morning. My heart pounded as I thought of him also reading the gospel, the Good News of Jesus Christ, which I had included, and prayed that God would soften his heart to receive Christ as his Lord and Savior.

It wasn't long before we received word that Bud had died. Our training with him was helpful and very enjoyable, but I knew without a doubt that God had had another purpose all along. *He was bringing me to Bud, not Bud to me.* God was offering Bud the Good News of the gospel through me because of Miki! The thought of it ran chills down my spine because up to that point, Miki's training had been the motive behind the choices I had made. But from then on, God confirmed the "hope" that I had always had within my heart that my horse, my riding, my training, everything that had to do with this wonderful gift He had given to me, was not for me, for my sake—but for Him. It was all for His Name's sake—for His glory—that others might come to know Him and enjoy the blessings of eternal life. "My Hope" took on a whole new eternal meaning, and so did the Scripture, *"Whether, then, you eat or drink or whatever you do, do all to the glory of God"* (1 Corinthians 10:31).

CHAPTER 8

Directed Steps

"The mind of man plans his way,
But the Lord directs his steps."
(Proverbs 16:9)

Our little riding group felt Bud's loss quite personally. As far as our sport was concerned, we were too sad for a while to pursue anyone else. We just sort of hacked around the trails wondering what we should do next.

One of the influences Bud had on me was the appreciation of good equipment. Up to that point, I hadn't understood much about saddles and bridles and just used what Barbara had so graciously loaned me. But Bud had a saddle that I thought was magnificent. It was German-made by George Kieffer that was worth about $1,800. Bud let me ride in it one day, and it made such a difference in my "seat" and my posture on Miki's back that I determined it would be my choice if I could ever afford one. *That'll be the day*, I thought—*O ye of little faith!*

As I drove into Burbank one Saturday morning to see Miki, I couldn't get the word "saddle" off my mind! A tack shop was close to the off-ramp of the freeway, so I made an impulsive decision to swing into the parking lot just to see what they had. Struggling to get a saddle into her trunk was a gal my age that I came to know as Mary. We nodded, and I said, "I hope that's not my saddle you're buying!" with a laugh.

"Well," she replied, "it's a Passier, a very expensive French saddle that my trainer wants me to try." Trainer? Did she say trainer? Suddenly I was less interested in her saddle.

Mary was proud to show me a flier that had just been made about her trainer, Kim Keenan-Staley, who was an accomplished International dressage rider, having trained in both California and Europe. Kim was at that time competing to be chosen for the Olympics and came out to Mary's barn in Santa Clarita once a week.

"Santa Clarita!" I shouted, "Where in Santa Clarita? I live out there, and I've been keeping my horse here in Burbank because I didn't know there were any boarding places or trainers out there," I bellowed! Mary giggled with delight as she saw my excitement and invited me out that very afternoon to watch her lesson at 2:30 and to meet Kim. She told me to keep the flier, popped the Passier into her trunk, and drove off. *Thank you, Lord,* I prayed. *That's why you directed me to come here!* I was still in an attitude of amazement as I walked through the back door of the store. *I may as well look at saddles anyway,* I thought.

Once inside, the shopkeeper, Buddy, whom I knew

well, began to show me various saddles and answered some of the questions I had. But I really didn't know what to ask! All I knew was that I liked the Kieffer, but I wasn't going to mention that because I knew how expensive it was. Buddy had several saddles displayed on wooden mounts, which I had fun sitting in one after another. They were from various countries, but my eyes didn't light up over any of them, and neither did his. He kept saying, "Nope, that's not right for you. Nope, not that one." Even the Passier that I knew was more expensive than the Kieffer was unacceptable for me according to Buddy's trained eye.

"Hold on, I've got just the saddle for you," he said. He pulled down off the shelf —you guessed it—a Kieffer saddle! Looking at a brand new one took my breath away: shiny black leather, soft and smooth, with awesome knee-pads that assist in keeping the rider's legs in their proper position on the horse's side. I had said nothing to Buddy that I already admired the Kieffer, but obediently sat in it. "This is a size eighteen," he said, "and although you're slender, you need this kind of room to move around in. I think it's perfect for you. How does it feel?" he asked. It felt great! It felt perfect!

I looked at him woefully, "I like it a lot, Buddy, but I'm afraid this one is out of my price range."

"Well, I'll make you an offer you can't refuse" (he probably graduated from the Dale Carnegie course on Good Salesmanship!). "I'll knock $300 off, and you take it and try it on your horse for a week to make sure it fits him too. If you don't like it, you don't have to buy it." What a deal! How could I turn it down? But I did. I couldn't run ahead of the Lord on a purchase like that; Frank and I needed to pray about it. I told Buddy thanks, but I would wait, which was fine with him. The offer would hold. I sucked in a gulp of air and left the shop. It was time to go see Miki and give him a ride anyway.

Later that afternoon, I decided to take Mary up on her offer to watch her lesson. I made my way out to Mary's barn in Santa Clarita—a back-road kind of place nestled in a canyon across a creek-bed—a real out-in-the-country kind of feel to it that I didn't know even existed. It was totally different than what I was accustomed to in the bustling city of Burbank. I eventually found it, watched the lesson, and wondered how it would all work out. Kim shook my hand as we met and said she would be happy to train Miki and me. I had my Burbank friends in mind too, and attempted to negotiate on their behalf so we could train as a group, but that was something she could not do. Burbank would be out of her way, and she was spread thin already. The training had to be at this barn... but how?

At that point, the barn owner/manager, Jan, asked if I'd like to have a look around. We walked the property, inspected the dressage arena together, talked about future plans for growth, and looked at the barn stalls and pipe corrals that had minimal cover. We discussed prices. I couldn't afford the barn stall, but the pipes were within reach. Jan sat down with me in her office and also made me an offer I couldn't refuse (it was that kind of day). She said she had one pipe left. She said I was the "kind of people" she liked to have at her facility, and she would hold that pipe for me for two weeks until I made a decision. It was the middle of April, so I had to decide by May 1.

I drove home bubbling over with news for Frank, with questions and decisions to be made. I told him the whole story—running into Mary, Buddy's saddle offer, meeting Kim as a possible trainer, followed by Jan's offer for stabling Miki closer to home. First, we prayed together, then we hopped right back into the car and drove back to the Santa Clarita barn. I wanted Frank to see it to help with this big decision to move Miki and start a whole new equestrian life away from everything Miki and I had known for many months, not to mention years for me. By the time we got back there, everyone was gone, so we sauntered around the place, even checking the restrooms. When we saw flowers in the men's room, we said, "That's it! If they care enough to put flowers in a men's restroom, they're going to care more about everything else—especially Miki." We laughed at our decision-making process and realized this could possibly be Miki's new home. But the real clincher was when we saw a Christian "fish" insignia on the sign at the entrance to the dirt road. Within the week, I called Jan and began to make all the arrangements necessary for the transport. And she confirmed her faith in Christ!

I only had to wait a day on the saddle, though, because Frank called me at work and said we had received $1,500 from our tax refund, and he wanted me to have it for the Kieffer saddle! I tried it on Miki, and it fit him perfectly. Frank and I rejoiced together, and I thanked God once again for my unselfish husband.

It was a time of God "directing my steps" that I'll never forget. And it was unbelievable moments of gratitude to Him for my husband, whose unselfishness toward me and my desires reflected the loving-kindness of our great God indwelling his heart. When we prayed together, we put God in charge: *"...for your heavenly Father knows that you need all these things. But seek first His kingdom and His righteousness; and all these things shall be added to you"* (Matthew 6:32-33, NKJV).

Shortly after arriving at the new barn, we made friends with Katie and her beautiful horse that was a nice match to Miki in coloring, and we entered the Newhall Fourth of July Parade together with me in my a "ten-gallon" hat! It was fun decorating our horses in red, white, and blue ribbons too. Miki was still a feisty baby at five years old who wanted to trot on the asphalt down the main street! Other than that, he handled the crowd, animated children with squirt guns, and banners like a champ!

Katie and I enjoyed many trail rides together along with another friend, Kris, who boarded across the road. These California hills were much more rugged and arid than the hills near Burbank or Hollywood. They were covered with sagebrush and wildflowers, with only a few trees for shade and fire-access roads that allowed us to climb to the top if we were brave enough. We did a couple of times, but we usually stayed down along the riverbed, which was desert-dry until the rainy season in the wintertime but, even then, I was able to get Miki to cross water thanks to Alan Hicks' previous training—unless it was too high! The main thing we needed to keep our eyes peeled for was rattlesnakes—fortunately, I personally never saw one, but the manager had anti-venom in the office fridge just in case, which unnerved me. Nonetheless, Miki maneuvered himself well in the new surroundings—and we enjoyed our new friends.

CHAPTER 9

Sent by Chance?

"So shall My Word be that goes forth from My mouth; It shall not return to Me void. But it shall accomplish what I please, And it shall prosper in the thing for which I sent it."
(Isaiah 55:11, NKJV)

After settling in for a year, I joined the Santa Clarita Valley chapter of the California Dressage Society (CDS), which is a non-profit, tax-exempt corporation and a group member organization of the United States Dressage Federation (USDF). CDS maintains a videotape library, defines insurance requirements, considers recognition of competitions, conducts education programs, and recognizes achievement through award programs for horse and rider. CDS believes that dressage competition is the ultimate test of training to determine the development of harmony between horse and rider and that all competitions and events should be conducted for the well-being and welfare of horses.

During our first show season in 1998 with Miki, I became a CDS "Qualified Riding Member," earning scores over 60 percent at First Level, and we were awarded a certificate which I gladly framed and hung on our wall.

We won several first-place blue ribbons.

That same year our picture appeared on the front page of "Dressage Letters" for having had the privilege of riding in a CDS European Instructor Clinic for Amateurs conducted by Belgian trainer Jan Dupont, who came to this country to share his European-bred expertise with American hopefuls.

The Dr. Reiner Klimke Symposium

One of the most privileged weekends of my entire horse life was my experience at the Klimke/Tellington-Jones Symposium at the Los Angeles Equestrian Center. This was the same Dr. Reiner Klimke that was sponsoring the clinic in which Fefe bolted, and I ended up in the dirt! Now perhaps I had the chance to save face (at least to myself!).

I was invited to ride in a special Saturday evening clinic that Linda Tellington-Jones was conducting alongside Dr. Klimke. Her specialty was TTEAM, **T**ellington-Jones **E**quine **A**wareness **M**ethod, which is *not* deep massage. On the contrary, an article in *Dressage Today*[ix] explains it as a system of touches and body-awareness techniques that bring the horse into "physical, mental and emotional balance. Its three pillars include TTouch bodywork, ground exercises, and riding with awareness. The TTouches bring new awareness on a cellular level to every part of the horse's body--literally waking up cells and releasing fear so the horse can be aware of his whole body. Then he is freer to feel a rider's aids and do what is asked." Her TTouch expertise was a form of physical manipulations that cause a horse to relax and be sensitized to its own muscles and extremities in order to use those muscles and/or extremities more effectively in any given movement. This allows him to think and not just react, making the horse freer to come to you instead of going away from you. Linda Tellington-Jones says,

> The horse will deal with the fear when he's under saddle by thinking about it instead of escaping it. We overcome the flight reflex by teaching the horse to stop and think when he's afraid.

She wanted three horses that were "different" from the dozen dressage horses that were riding in the Klimke clinics. Miki was definitely different, so a friend referred me to her, and I was invited. A day-pass for Saturday was granted to me, and I thoroughly enjoyed learning vicariously as dressage riders of varying levels were put through their paces with their valiant steeds at the instruction of the "master," Reiner Klimke himself. He patiently directed them through his thick German accent, enhancing each pair's strengths and finding ways to help them overcome their weaknesses. Sometimes he would instruct a rider to take their stirrups away to help them sit in the saddle with suppleness and balance, without relying on the irons for support. A quote from *A Festival of Dressage* magazine says:

> If, for example, a dressage rider turns out one foot more than another, it means their seat bones will be at different angles, their weight unevenly distributed and the horse's movements would be affected.[x]

Most importantly, it was heart-warming to witness that he always had the horse's best interest and enjoyment in mind. After all, a happy horse makes a more willing athlete. Dr. Klimke stressed that "nothing is ever accomplished in an atmosphere of fear. As soon as a horse experienced discomfort and seemed ready to say 'no,' both Klimke and Tellington-Jones would back off. But then they would return and in a non-threatening manner again asking the horse for a little more trust." He would say, "Relax. Let your horses come back to nature. Tell him what you want, and then leave him alone."

At the break, I approached Linda and introduced myself to thank her for the opportunity to work with her. Her warm and gracious spirit made me feel like the thrill was *hers* (believe me, it was all *mine*), and she asked if she could come see Miki. I pulled him out of the stall, and she started doing some of the routine TTouch on him, and a small crowd gathered around. Miki responded to her acceptingly. She asked me to write down the areas in which I was having some difficulty with him, like the struggle I had in getting him into the bridle and his difficulty in picking up the left lead canter. She said she would work on those in the clinic that evening. Then she informed me that she would be asking Dr. Klimke to come into the clinic because she thought Miki was so pretty that she wanted him to see us! I was in shock, to say the least, and yet awe-struck to think that my equestrian "idol" would actually know that we existed! What an honor!

Just riding in the Equidome at LAEC again with an audience of approximately 1,200 spectators gathered from as far away as New Zealand was exciting and intimidating alike! I was a much more accomplished rider by this time since my day of bailing off Fefe years earlier, but was still feeling a bit nervous knowing we were under Klimke's watchful eye! The Equidome was all lit up with the beautiful dressage arena in the middle surrounded by fuchsia-colored flowers. Linda was finishing up on another horse, so I proceeded to ride Miki around the perimeter, putting him through some walk-trot transitions, attempting to keep his attention away from all of the distractions going on. It was a lot to ask a horse to endure if he hadn't been seasoned in the show arenas because of the noises all around us—some people moving about and the bright lights glistening. He did rather well despite feeling strong in my hands—certainly, he was also aware of the nerves I was attempting to stifle but, nevertheless, transmitting to him.

Linda asked me to demonstrate the left lead canter, which I had indicated to her was a struggle for him. Was it his problem or mine since he was able to pick up the right canter lead with no problem? I struggled to keep him rounded and in his proper frame at a rhythmic gait. As we started out, I felt like I was "all thumbs" because I couldn't keep from thinking that Dr. Klimke was there watching us! Then she asked me to dismount, and we pulled the saddle and bridle off. She began working her fingers in his mouth, then moved to his stomach, gently pushing up with her fingers and causing him to raise his back and lower his head. She also worked on pulling and manipulating his tail and palpating his legs. Miki's eyes became glazed as he thoroughly relaxed, enjoying her "touches" for which she was renowned. I was also given very practical advice by her team on how his bridle should fit, my spurs were removed, and certain other riding adjustments were made. We re-saddled, I re-mounted, and Miki was almost immediately better as we picked up the left lead canter. I was thrilled.

The next morning when I went to bridle Miki, he was much more accepting of the bit, and when I worked him, he was as smooth as glass—neck stretched down, lighter on the bit. All I can say is that I felt like Miki was "rescued" from painful or unknowing mistakes I was making so that he and I both would have more of a chance to advance in our riding with better communication between us. I was learning to "listen to his whispers," as Linda put it.

All of the riders, including myself, were invited to have a photoshoot with Dr. Klimke and Linda. I marveled at the opportunity just to be there! I strolled over on Miki alongside one of the Grand Prix riders who had had a wonderful lesson with Dr. Klimke. I enjoyed the privilege of having a professional photoshoot with everyone and returned Miki to his stall for his leftover breakfast. Unfortunately, the photos were later lost, and we never got to see them, but the memory of the moment lingers still.

Later that day, during their autograph session, Linda once again made me feel like *she* was delighted to see *me* again (a good lesson on "how to win friends!") and took me with her up to the *front* of the long line to autograph a book for me. I was also able to get Dr. Klimke's autograph as the two of them sat me at the table between them. Others actually took photographs of the three of us, shoulder to shoulder. What an amazing delight that was for me. At that point,

I offered Dr. Klimke and Linda each my *Mikwaiti "My Hope"* booklet with my and Miki's picture on the cover to remember me by, which I autographed for them, and they were gracious to take them from me.

Suddenly, the people waiting in line started asking for an autographed copy from me as well and told me how beautiful they thought Miki was and how much they enjoyed my ride from the previous evening. What a humbling moment, and what a quiet joy for me to know each one would be reading the Good News in my booklet with an invitation to receive Jesus as their Lord and Savior. Indeed, weeks later, I received a note from the gal who took the above picture saying how blessed she had been by the gospel message in the booklet.

What made that moment most significant was not just

my opportunity to meet Dr. Reiner Klimke and Linda Tellington-Jones. Yes, we shook hands, we spoke, and I was star-truck, to say the least, but, more importantly, I hoped they would be reading my booklet as well. I was in awe of what I had just experienced. I could only thank God for the gift He had given me with Miki; and I was so grateful to Priscilla Mason, the CDS Chapter Chair of Antelope Valley, for calling me and giving me this incredible opportunity; but my special thanks went to Linda for the dedication and warmth she extended to me and all of the riders. No wonder animals loved her. People did too! And I, for one, was committed to learning more about TTouch and how it benefitted our horses from the ground up. Listen, if Klimke thought she was the best—then so did I!

Little did anyone know that six months later, we would each receive a letter from Linda with the sad news that, without warning, Dr. Klimke would be dead from a heart attack. It was a shock to the worldwide equestrian community. However, because of Mikwaiti, I have "hope" that he was able to read my booklet and possibly respond to the Spirit of God's invitation to salvation—since it was that Spirit who had orchestrated this divine encounter between us in the first place! Absolutely amazing—another "God-incidence"—there is *no* coincidence in the life of a child of God!

God had given me a love for people and a burden for others to know Him. The greatest joy of my heart was to be able to hand out my testimony booklet to the riders and other wonderful people I met at barns, horse shows, etc. Perhaps, as a result of my horse and my booklet, Dr. Klimke, Linda, and the others would be drawn by the Lord into a saving knowledge of Him. All because of Mikwaiti, "My Hope."

CHAPTER 10

A Different Kind of Discipline

"Behold, how happy is the man
whom God reproves,
So do not despise the discipline of the Almighty.
For He inflicts pain, and gives relief;
He wounds, and His hands also heal.
From six troubles He will deliver you,
Even in seven evil will not touch you."
(Job 5:17-19)

I had been riding Miki nearly every day since the Symposium, and we enjoyed continuing to win first and second places in our First Level competitions together. He had great potential, and we were preparing to show our first Second Level test when that left front foot began to show signs of weakness again.

At first, beginning in January, I discovered he was "off" and called out a couple of vets to examine him. Finally, it was decided he needed x-rays. We discovered a gravel tract tunneling its way up inside the hoof wall of his front left foot, inflaming the sensitive laminae, much like the tender tissue or the quick underneath one's fingernail. Interestingly enough, the vet said it had been there a long time—so long, in fact, that the inflammation had leached calcium from the coffin bone inside the foot! This, then, was also making the bone sensitive. In most cases, when a horse has a gravel tract inside its hoof, it becomes infected and extremely obvious because it's very painful until the infection actually erupts through the top of the hoof (coronet band), lets off the pressure, and can be cleaned out. I was, at least, thankful that Miki had not had an infection and the acute pain that accompanies it. But without the infection, the condition went on for so long that the loss of calcium from the bone in his foot was serious! Could that have been the cause of the initial weakness in that foot when I first got him, that for at least three years, no one had ever discovered until now? If so, for that, I could rejoice because the vet said the prognosis was good. We could carve away the hoof (not a painful thing for the horse, sort of like cutting our fingernails, but something that would compromise the integrity of the hoof wall for a while). He would open up the tunnel and just let the air dry it up as the hoof continued to grow back. But once the hoof grew out again, he should be as good as new. That would take time, however, and it meant absolutely no riding. So I hand-walked and medicated Miki for many months. Finally, a "green light" from the vet put us back to work. I was ecstatic, feeling like all our problems were over. Not so fast!

His first day back under saddle, as I rode him at a walk down to the arena, he planted that same foot on a big rock in the road and seemed to twist his ankle. He was limping again, so I babied him for another two weeks! But why was that foot still so sensitive to normal use? He had stepped on many rocks before. The question haunted me.

After a couple of weeks, he seemed better, and I thought we were on our way back to normal. However, one morning I discovered he had been bitten by a huge, black horsefly in a tender area which caused him to be swollen and very sore. So, we gave him a shot and let him stand another week. Why was God keeping us from getting back into our routine? I cried out to Him often. The Bible says, *"Hope deferred makes the heart sick"* (Proverbs 13:12), and that was exactly how I felt—heartsick.

Then for several weeks thereafter, we struggled through various philosophies of shoeing the horse from farriers whose opinions greatly differed. That came as a surprise to me, and it was hard to know who was right. The biggest clue, of course, was the horse's comfort level while being ridden. We tried everything, and, finally, we were back to work (by this time, it was August) with what seemed to be balanced shoeing, although he was being supported by pads, wedges, and other paraphernalia that he had never needed before! But we had missed out on finishing that year's show season.

Finally, we had a long-awaited training lesson—nothing too strenuous, just a time of guiding us through proper equitation. As a reward, I took him out on the trail, which he loved, and slowly sauntered along a pretty path between a couple of cottonwood trees. All of a sudden, Miki's right front leg disappeared into a deep hole! A gopher hole, no doubt, but a mighty big gopher! Neither of us saw it coming. He quickly pulled himself out of it with me still on his back, and I was grateful he hadn't broken his leg! However, the next few days revealed that the bad step with his right leg had forced all of his weight on that susceptible front left foot, and it was sore again. Hoping he would bounce back from this too, I put him on Bute (horse aspirin), let him stand a few days, and kept hand walking him. But weeks went by, and he wasn't getting any better! What was the Lord trying to tell me about that left front foot? The disappointment was almost unbearable, and the frustration of not knowing what else to do was scary. It was getting to where I was afraid to bring him out of his stall again.

The counsel of friends convinced me to have a radioactive bone scan done on the leg, and, sure enough, his coffin bone was severely inflamed. That was the already-compromised bone inside the hoof wall that had lost calcium, basically at the very bottom of the leg that bears all the weight. But the vet gave me another clue. That particular foot grew a taller heel than his other foot did. Some farriers allowed it to grow tall naturally, whereas others would take it down only a little so as not to over-stretch the ligaments in the leg. But the x-rays and bone scan revealed that the tall heel caused the coffin bone to slant at an incorrect angle, pointing downward on the soft tissue inside the foot rather than providing a level weight-bearing surface, always making it susceptible to trauma and inflammation. "Cut that heel down drastically and make that bone level, and keep it down! Wrap the leg to support the ligaments so they won't become sore as a result"—were my orders from two vets! And the gravel tract was starting to come back despite the fact that I thought the various farriers were cleaning it out and keeping an eye on it!

I was so grateful to the Lord for this revelation—something He relentlessly pursued until we saw it in black and white! If all the other little accidents hadn't happened to that foot, the insidious gravel tract and tilted coffin bone could have possibly crippled Miki to an irreparable point where some people would have considered putting him down. People do that, you know. Horses are expensive to keep. And sometimes, if a horse is not able to be used for its intended function, it is destroyed. I wouldn't even let my mind go there. That was not ever going to be an option for me, even if he ended up being just a "lawn ornament" for the rest of his life. He was a keeper!

Other well-meaning friends suggested I sell Miki and buy another show-quality horse because they could see my frustration at not being able to get him well enough to ride consistently, much less for training and the show circuit. But just the thought of that brought sudden waves of sadness. Miki was too special to be dismissed so lightly. He was God's gift to me! Surely the Lord was not going to abandon him now, and neither would I. It's not as though his problems were totally genetic and/or degenerative (notwithstanding the heel problem which was aggravated by human error) or that there was no light at the end of the tunnel. I could see the light, and I still had hope for him—for us. I couldn't give up on him now after a year of struggling that was leading to a solution. So, I concluded in my heart that Miki and I were together for life, Lord willing. But if I had to put him in a pasture in the prime of his life where I would not be able to ride him anymore, it would break my heart. Needless to say, I stormed the gates of heaven with thanksgiving for revealing the hidden cause of his subtle lameness after all these years, and with more prayer for his complete recovery, as did many of my Christian friends and family on our behalf!

The vet told me not to expect the horse to be sound for the remainder of the year. That was October, and he had already been out of commission off and on for ten months! Continual medication twice a day, hand-walking, ride-walking, with frequent vet calls, corrective shoeing, and the grace of God eventually brought Miki to a point of wellness after a total of fifteen months of virtual lay-up.

He began to feel fairly good again, and I let my hopes get high. The weather was clearing up, the sun was coming out on a consistent basis, and he and I were happy to be riding again. A spring show was approaching in three weeks, and, with light practice, I figured entering him into one lower-level class would be safe. But then he was so fresh from being cooped up, he bucked and twisted during our lesson, and he threw his back out!

I learned one thing for sure—rehabilitating a horse that has been out of commission for a long period of time, as Miki had been, is a real challenge. Often their mind and their "wind" are way ahead of their muscles and ligaments. They think they're fine, kick up their heels, and end up re-injuring themselves somewhere else.

With all the enthusiasm on hold, the discipline of being laid up was painful, not just physically for him or financially for us, but emotionally for me. Once again, I had an opportunity to lean on what the Bible says, for example, in Hebrews 12:11: *"All discipline for the moment seems not to be joyful, but sorrowful; yet to those who have been trained by it afterwards it yields the peaceful fruit of righteousness."*

The relentless "discipline" of training and all that goes with it, getting up extra early, trying to juggle my schedule between my family, chosen vocation, sport, and the discipline of caring for a lame horse (all the hand-walking, the anxious moments of not knowing exactly where he hurt or why, the vet bills, etc.) seemed "sorrowful" at times. But I had confidence that the rewards would far outweigh the trial or test because I had learned time and time again that *"All things work together for good to those who love God"* (Romans 8:28, KJV). This promise from the Bible would result in my eternal enjoyment in heaven as I am molded and conformed to the image of Christ here on the earth through the day-to-day endurance of praying, trusting, and waiting. I knew that someday this time of waiting in my life would "yield the peaceful fruit" or reward of "righteousness." After all, *Mikwaiti* not only means "to wait," it also means "to hope in." When there is hope in God, waiting becomes easier. And maybe someday for Miki, the waiting would make him totally sound again. It certainly was teaching me patience and trust as I watched God weave together all of the circumstances with my good and His glory in mind.

In the Christian life, sometimes it's a real effort to live God's way, the way the Bible tells us to with trust and patience, without grumbling and complaining. It would seem so much easier at times to do things our own way instead. But that would be like sitting on the back of a runaway horse (like Fefe)—no control, no direction, no purpose, pattern, or beauty. The end is fear and calamity. But when God lovingly disciplines the Christian, surrender to His perfect will brings fulfillment and peace. All we have to do is wait… and never lose hope.

CHAPTER 11

Tobiah ~
"The Goodness of Jehovah"

*"For I will turn their mourning to joy, will
comfort them, And make them rejoice rather than
sorrow… And My people shall be satisfied with
My goodness, Says the Lord."*
(Jeremiah 31:13-14, NKJV)

I was trying not to have a heavy heart that lovely spring
Sunday after church when Frank and I went to a horse
show to give moral support to my girlfriend, Joy, who was
showing her beautiful Dutch Warmblood horse, Hunter. I
began that morning with a prayer and asked God for His
encouragement. I would need it because Joy had worked
hard to get ready for this "spring fling," and she was excited; I wanted to be excited with her. Indeed, I was proud of
her and Hunter for their accomplishments as a team. But
Miki and I had been practicing for that particular show too
when he had sprained his back. It's no wonder I was feeling depressed, but I was hiding it—I didn't want Joy to see
anything except my enthusiasm for her.

Several of us were gathered around the warm-up arena watching Joy and Hunter prepare for their competition when someone said, "There's Hilda Gurney." Hilda always remembered giving me a lesson on Masquerade (Miki) when I rode him for the first time. She had just shown another pinto that I suspected was related to Miki. I called out to her and asked if that was a "Modern baby" (Miki's sire) she was riding? "It sure is," she exclaimed (so it was Miki's beautiful half-brother), "and Barbara is here too!" As she rode on by, Barbara and I spotted each other, and she greeted Frank and me with a warm hug. We hadn't seen her in several years.

She caught me off guard when she asked with a grin, "How's Miki?" Barbara knew me well, and she knew the horse well, and I just couldn't hold it back any longer—not from her. I started to cry. Now I caught her off guard! "He's not dead, is he?" she asked, almost in shock. "No, no," I sniveled, to which she showed great relief. But I began to recount the horrendous last fifteen months of unfortunate circumstances and unsuccessful rehabilitation.

I told Barbara that I had called three of my trainers in a moment of desperation, asking if any of them knew of a show horse I could possibly half-lease, just to keep up my equitation training in dressage. The years of riding and training so far had given me muscle memory that I didn't want to lose, to which any athlete can relate, just as a horse loses his muscle when he's in lay-up. That way, I could rehab Miki very, very slowly without worrying about getting him ready to show, but just concentrate on getting him well. None of them, however, could come up with any suggestions… but, of course, Barbara did. In fact, without hesitation, she offered me not just one horse but a choice from among three horses, which I could just take over—no lease, nothing. This beloved friend, once again, had been used by God to show me unselfish love and had instantly lifted my burden.

Ol' What's His Name?

One of the horses she described stood out as the most desirable. His name was BBC ("Barbara's Black Colt," she said, for lack of a better name). He was a seventeen-hand Trakehner-Saddlebred mix, all black, and showing the following weekend at First and Second Levels. "Why don't you come see him show, and if you like him, you can take him. You can even change his name," she said.

Since I'm tall, a seventeen-hand horse sounded perfect, especially since I had ridden Fefe, who was 17.2 hands. And the Trakehner breed is a warmblood from Russia, tailor-made for dressage. Plus, First and Second Levels were right where Miki and I had left off, so I could pick up with BBC and maybe eventually take him on to Third and Fourth Levels. I felt like I was being blessed by God right on the spot. I knew, right then and there, that if this horse was to be a part of God's will for me, I would give him a name that would honor God, just like I had done with Mik-waiti. This would be my gesture of Thanksgiving because God was using this moment to encourage my heart as I had requested.

I did go to watch BBC show two days in a row. The first time I saw him, I admired him. He was big, black, and beautiful. His rider, Kayla, was a young seven-teen-year-old, and she handled him masterfully. They did well together, and he took first and third places in his tests.

Barbara made the arrangements for Kayla (who had three other horses to ride) and me to get together the following Tuesday morning, very early, so she could school me during my first ride with BBC. I was somewhat intimidated by his size and reminiscent of what it had felt like to be on Fefe's back, with his neck so far out in front of me that I couldn't even reach his ears if I tried (which I didn't!). But remember, Fefe had been the "gentle giant." BBC was different. He had a reputation for being finicky. He wasn't a push-button horse. Oh, he knew the training all right, but he expected his riders to know what they were doing, or else he pinned his ears back, bucked, and tried to get them off (with some success, I had heard). I had no clue what he would think of me, nor me of him. I mounted with a feeling of caution and a silent prayer for the Lord's help. I had had many experiences with Miki's wild antics as he was growing up to draw from, but this was a mature-minded horse with a huge body and a dif-ferent kind of temperament.

My instincts told me just to take it real slow. I told myself, *Keep a loose rein, let him walk at first, keep my legs
off, use no spurs, don't be too demanding so that I don't
draw attention to myself. Just sort of blend in with the
saddle. Maybe he won't notice it's me instead of Kayla;* I
privately chuckled. Besides, Kayla was there in the ring to
help keep him calm.

To my surprise, he seemed to like the way we began.
He didn't watch me constantly (a horse can look backward
180 degrees with just the tilt of its head and can see the
rider in the saddle). Everywhere his eye looked, his ear followed. So, I could tell he wasn't preoccupied with this new
person occupying his back because his ears weren't backward but were pointing to the front or to the sides (horses
are animals of prey, so God made it possible for them to
look in two directions at once, out both sides of their head).
Since he wasn't looking back at me too much—I thought
that was a good sign.

Soon it was time to attempt our first trot. Would he
go forward, or would he evade my signal and slack off?
Surprisingly, there was no battle there either. He moved
forward nicely, but his gaits were huge! That was going to
take some getting used to on my part. I was going to have
to establish my timing and balance with his way of moving,
and he covered a lot of ground fast!

All in all, we hit it off well, and I rode him consistently
for three or four days, took a break due to rain, and started

back again. I was told that sometimes it could be difficult to get him to canter; yet, he picked up his canter leads for me as I asked for them—no evading, no bucking. I was very surprised. Barbara was glad I was riding him well and even coached me a couple of times. My gratitude went to the Lord first who was answering my daily prayer for protection, and then to her for her continual care and generosity toward me.

But was I getting overly excited too soon? Was this really going to be my new show horse? Some other things needed to fall into place first. Would my husband still be in agreement? Could we afford to board two horses knowing how expensive even one horse is to maintain? Where would I keep him, and if I put him with Miki, would they get along or end up hurting one another? I wanted only the Lord's will in this decision, not my own. I prayed about each hurdle, then put "feet" to my prayers and began my investigation.

First of all, I spoke to my barn manager, Jan, about boarding and cost. What if I put BBC into Miki's 24 x 24 pipe corral, dividing it in half to two 12 x 24 paddocks— would she allow that, and what would she charge me? She was happy for me, knowing that I needed to rehabilitate Miki very slowly, and this would provide a good mount for me to train and be trained on in the meantime. She gave me nothing but positive affirmation and said she would help me acclimate the horses and would only charge me for any extra food that BBC ate, but no extra board. That was encouraging and made it economically possible. That was prayer-hurdle number one out of the way!

In fact, in a bolt out of the blue one Saturday, we came up with a plan to take a twenty-four-foot, four-rail pipe with a gate and just ran it down the center to make the two 12 x 24 pipe stalls. BBC was only in a 10 x 10 stall at that time, so a 12 x 24 would give him plenty of room and, most importantly, would provide the protection between the two horses. With the gate, I could easily go between them. I thought Miki would love the company. He really was quite social and compliant with other horses. So, that was the second prayer answered; two hurdles down.

I told Barbara about the boarding arrangements, and she absolutely approved; however, how could I afford more shoeing and vet bills (if necessary)? Barbara offered to take those responsibilities since I would pay for his (and my) training and showing. That expense had already been allocated for Miki, which I didn't think would materialize at least for another year since we were back to light exercise only. So, hurdle number three was knocked down as that prayer was answered!

With the economic hurdles out of the way and knowing the sad frustration I had been experiencing, Frank was, once again, supportive of the plan. That was the biggest confirmation of all because our desire was for us to always be unified in major decision-making. Once again, God graciously revealed His will to me through the counsel of my husband. The green lights were everywhere—and I moved through them with joy!

The final barrier was BBC himself. Was he really the one for me? Would we be a good match? Was I willing to take on a horse like him that was really going to keep me on my toes—or better yet, could I? I voiced my fear and trepidation to some of the girls at the barn who knew the horse fairly well and, to a person, each one assured me that what was developing between us was a good thing, not to be deterred, and their enthusiasm lightened my heart. As a result, I was able to share my story about the answers to my prayer with several people. Already they were changing his name from BBC ("Barbara's Black Colt") to PBC ("Pat's Black Colt"). *No,* I thought to myself, *his name will be special, something to reflect the continual goodness of God in my life, even by providing one horse after another.*

With the final decision having been made, going to pick up BBC at the appointed time was not something to take lightly. In fact, I felt rather nervous about it. Number one, I don't like to trailer alone—it's always safer to go on the "buddy system" just in case something happens. But I had taken a vacation day off work, and Frank wasn't available to help me, so off I went, gassed up, hooked up, prayed up, and drove the thirty-plus miles to Burbank.

At my destination was a different story. All my new friends (and old ones) were there to greet me and help get the horse loaded into the trailer. I had a "warmblood" sized trailer by that time—extra tall, a little roomier—and I was wondering how this giant of a horse would fit. He did—just barely! Barbara loaded him for me, and I carefully watched her technique. He boarded with some minor coaxing, and we were ready to roll, despite the fact that my double tires were looking a little flat on that side! His ears actually touched the roof of the trailer stall, and we had to squeeze the "butt" bar into place behind him. He was in without an inch to spare!

I had asked some of the gals to come with us, especially Kayla, so that she could ride him at my barn to help him feel more secure and acclimated. My friend, Sandy, came along for the ride too. I felt better about having them follow along behind me, again, just for the security of having help if I needed it on the road and to share in the joy of the occasion.

After we all arrived safely in Santa Clarita, BBC unloaded quite nicely, and I could tell he had done his fair share of being hauled from place to place. So, I was glad I didn't have to put that kind of effort into training him for the trailer. Training a horse to load and unload in a trailer is crucial, not only for the sake of showing but more importantly if one needs to take their horse to the vet or even in case of a fire or some other natural disaster or emergency. Horses that won't load within a short amount of time might get left behind. That's why Frank and I had invested in a trailer for Miki since we were now so far away from Barbara's barn, where everything I had needed through the years had been so generously provided.

We took BBC over to the crossties and began the process of saddling him up for his first ride and a look-see around the property. I was grateful Kayla was there because he was comfortable with her, and I could tell that just her presence made him feel relaxed. It can be very distressing for a horse to be moved around; they can become disoriented and even depressed. This "first impression" that he was having of these new surroundings was very important. Kayla climbed on his back and carefully sauntered him down to the dressage arena. He was staring at every new tree, bush, neighboring horses, and buildings, but he felt secure in Kayla's confident hands.

She rode him around the arena for about twenty minutes, just enough time to get him warmed up, and then invited me to get on him. Why was I feeling nervous? I had ridden the horse for a month. We had built a respectful relationship. But he still intimidated me a bit because of his size and disposition, and having him in this new surrounding made me just as nervous as it made him. But I tried not to show it because he would be able to feel my hesitancy the second I sat in the saddle. So, I took a deep breath and climbed up. Of course, he was fine, and so was I. We had a good short ride, and I felt like we had been able to get our feet wet together before we were left entirely on our own.

After a quick shower in the wash rack, he was ready to meet his new "brother," Miki, and take up residence in his beautiful new pipe corral. The three of us walked him up to the pipes, and I led him into his corral. There was only the pipe rail separating the two horses; nothing else to prevent them from getting at each other. I took off his halter, quickly exited the stall, latched the gate, and held my breath. My previous observation of BBC was that he was definitely an alpha in relation to other horses, and Miki was more compliant, so I honestly was a little afraid for Miki's safety. Would BBC bite him, would he strike out with his front legs, would he turn and kick with his back legs? We waited.

The two horses quickly approached each other, puffing their necks up in a show of strength, bringing their heads together in what almost looked like a horse-hug, as they snorted and sniffed each other with nostrils flaring. Miki was the first to squeal. After all, it had been his territory that he was now sharing with this big stranger. But that was it. That was all. One squeal and then instant friends! I couldn't believe my eyes and rejoiced in my heart at another answer to prayer. I didn't know what I would have done if they hadn't gotten along.

The boys

Kayla and Sandy knew that their job was done; we had accomplished our goals without a hitch. They gave BBC one last pat on the neck, gave me a warm hug, and drove off. I turned back to the stalls with tears in my eyes and said to BBC, "I christen thee *Tobiah*, which means 'the goodness of Jehovah' because you have been given to me as a blessing from the Lord in answer to my plea for comfort. Together, we will endeavor to bring glory to God. Welcome to your new home!" The nickname "Toby" quickly stuck with everyone around the barn.

A Scary Reminder

Up to this point, I hadn't really understood the delicacy

of a horse's emotions—Miki's, that is. Just three days after Toby arrived, Miki gave me another scare. It was his turn to work, and he seemed a little lazy as he stood in his stall, not anxious to get out. It was hot, and I didn't really feel like working either. But we do what we must. So, I pulled him out, groomed him, mounted up, and off we went to the arena.

Our basic routine usually consisted of a fifteen-minute walk ride just to give him time to warm up and stretch out his muscles. Then I would put him into a trot while I rose in the saddle every other stride (called posting) to give his back time to warm up and keep my weight from making it sore. Our typical routine during his rehab was to go four times around the circumference of the arena in one direction, across the diagonal, and then four times in the other direction. That took about ten minutes. Then I'd let him walk one lap to stretch out his neck muscles again that had been kept taut as he "rounded" for me on the bit. After a brief resting walk, it was time for the canter warm-up. This was another twenty minutes of four times around the arena in both directions, except I would add in a twenty-meter circle at each end and one in the middle. We finished up with a final ten-minute walk ride to let him cool down and prevent any muscle cramping. Miki worked well for me that morning.

I took him back to his stall after a refreshing shower (for him, not me!) and felt good about the work he had done. One last item in our routine—I always gave him five lumps of sugar. In fact, I couldn't even say the word "sugar," or else he would be sniffing each hand and every pocket trying to find it! He always knew he would get his sugar lumps after every ride. In fact, there were times in the past I almost forgot and had to double back because he looked forward to it so much.

I gave him his first three lumps, and he chewed and licked and eventually spat them out of his mouth. What? Never, not in four years, did he ever do that! My heart skipped a beat. I studied the expression on his face. Something was wrong. Crying out to the Lord in my heart, I ran for help, and the only one still there was my close friend, Katie. With alarm on my face and panic in my voice, I told her my concern for Miki. As usual, she dropped everything and came to our aid. She told me she had just learned the day before how to use a rectal thermometer on a horse to take its temperature. She ran to get it, and we started examining him for other symptoms. She masterfully inserted the thermometer, tying it off on the tail so it wouldn't get "lost," notifying me that the normal temperature of most horses was around 99-101 degrees. While we waited, I took Miki's digital pulse in the soft tissue of his front leg. In ten seconds, I counted twelve beats. Multiply that by six—that made seventy beats per minute! That was high. Normal should be around forty or less because he was done working and was rested, even cooled by the shower. Katie explained that a high pulse meant the horse was probably in pain or distress. We removed the thermometer, and Miki had a temperature of 101 degrees, the high side of normal. We concluded he was sick! Our first thought was the dreaded "C" word—colic. We put our ears up to Miki's rotund belly to listen for gut sounds (a horse's digestive system never stops working and making noises). There was silence. Not a good sign!

I have been told that colic feels like having severe gas pains that can't be relieved. Actually, there is a lot of gas built up because it is blocked by some kind of impaction in the intestines. It can mean agony, sometimes surgery, and sometimes death for the horse. Miki also acted nauseated and, since horses can't vomit, he could get no relief from his nausea either. Once we realized how sick he was, it became evident in his demeanor. Every time I moved across the stall, he would come to me and bury his head in my chest. His eyes were half-mast and sad-looking. His facial expression was one of distress. How had I missed all this before? I felt cruel for having ridden him. If only he could have told me, but I was finally "listening to his whispers," as Linda had taught me.

As usual, God was right there with us in stall number forty-nine. He had not abandoned us nor forsaken us (Hebrews 12:6). Katie recalled that Dr. Marteney, whose practice was a good thirty miles north in Acton and was normally so swamped that he was difficult to retain on a moment's notice, just *happened* to have an appointment that day at the barn across the road from us, and a quick call to our mutual friend, Kris, verified that. She gave me Marteney's number, and within minutes, I had him on the phone. He advised me to give the horse a shot of Banamine, which would act as a muscle-relaxant and help to alleviate some of the discomforts, and also feed him a warm bran mash that would work as a laxative. He would then be there within the hour.

I also called Frank for prayer—we always went to the Lord together when our emotions were shaken about something—and he was there in twenty minutes.

Kris came right over. Not only did she have the Banamine stored in her refrigerator, but she also knew how to give the intra-muscular shot into Miki's neck. Then we went back to her barn and prepared the warm bran mash. It was the consistency of a thick cream of wheat, except it was made of rice bran. Kris added a smidge of molasses for a sweeter taste and even cut up some apples. I knew Miki would love it. The doctor said that we should let him eat as much of it as he could until he could get there. But Miki didn't want it. He stuck his nose into the bucket and got some on his muzzle. Sadly, I knew he wanted to eat it, but his nausea was overpowering. My heart was breaking for him.

Finally, Dr. Marteney arrived and said he would have to oil the horse with mineral oil. There's only one way to do that—stick a long tube through his big nostril, down his long throat (which he would be forced to swallow), and into his stomach. Then the oil would be pumped in and would eventually work its way through his entire digestive tract until it lubricated and dislodged whatever was blocking the output. But Miki would have none of it.

I've taken dogs and cats to the vet and watched unpleasant procedures on them as the vet's assistant held them down, knowing that it was for their own good. But watching this horse struggle to prevent the doc from sticking this hose up his nose was traumatic. The doctor finally had to sedate him to where he looked like he would fall over, but he still had the presence of mind to throw his head up and keep from swallowing the tube. The vet was afraid Miki was going to leap on top of us in his panic, so he put him behind the pipe rail with us on the other side, so if he leaped, he would hit the rail and not us. The vet had been trampled that way once before, he said. I could hardly stand watching. I cried out in my heart for the Lord's help.

The vet then remembered he had a thinner tube in his truck. He said some vets didn't carry a tube that thin, but it was a good thing he did *(Thank you, Lord!)*. Within a few minutes, he had gotten Miki to swallow the thinner tube and was quickly sending the oil through it into his gut. What a relief! Now all we had to do was wait. Wait for manure.

By that time, it was early evening, and Frank and I were prepared to spend the night with the horse. Dr. Marteney said not to that we should go home and get a good night's rest. If all went well, Miki would get some relief within twelve to twenty-four hours. We did go home, but my eyes popped open at 6:00 a.m., and I drove like a madwoman back to the barn.

I never thought I would be so happy to see manure in my life! There it was, two piles worth, and Miki was eating! I opened up the gate and hung on his neck for an undetermined amount of time, thanking God for His mercy on this dependent creature. I called the vet and told him the happy news. He said we had caught it in time. Some people think, "Oh, he'll get over it by morning," without calling a vet, and by morning the horse is totally impacted and sometimes beyond hope.

If I hadn't tried to feed Miki his sugar, I would have gone home that afternoon and left him there—dangerously ill. I began to thank God for all the circumstances that He had brought together to bring us through this crisis, like having Dr. Marteney on his way to the barn nearby even before I called him. He, himself, was surprised by that turn of events since his practice was so far away, and he was glad that he "just happened" to be headed to an appointment *across the street* with Kris when we needed him. Not only was Katie very helpful with her newly learned thermometer skill, but I thanked God for having her there when everyone else had already gone and for her total unselfishness by staying with me and helping during those crucial hours. And then she *just happened* to know Dr. Marteney's schedule!

Kris's supplies on hand, her expertise in giving the shot,

her generosity with everything she had at her disposal, and her moral support made me think of her as an angel in disguise. Dr. Marteney's thinner oiling tube and Miki's quick recovery all added together to spell G-o-d C-a-r-e-s. We even had the discussion that the ride I put Miki through prior to discovering his illness was probably good for him in the long run. It kept things moving and possibly prevented a tighter blockage. I didn't feel like such a cruel mother after all.

Most importantly was my husband's prayer support—ever ready, on the scene, carrying my heart away from the problem at hand straight into the throne room of our God.

I let Miki rest from his ordeal for a few days before I brought him out of the stall again. This was a reminder, however, of why I had brought Toby home in the first place. Miki had been so fragile for a year and a half, and even though his leg finally seemed sound, he was still susceptible to other problems. I thanked God once again for giving me Toby to train on so that Miki could recuperate at his own pace. But I also realized that Miki somehow felt threatened by this new intruder into his paddock, especially at feeding time as I began to observe that Toby became aggressive at those times. I needed to pay extra attention to Miki—feed him first, talk to him first, pet him first—until he could feel more secure. I hoped I had made the right decision putting him and Toby together. I had no other easy choice now.

Fahrenheit Revisited

Becoming acclimated to Toby being at my barn was every bit as much an adjustment for me as it was for Miki. Granted, it was much easier to have both horses in one location rather than riding Toby at Burbank in the morning before work and then traveling thirty miles to Santa Clarita after work to tend to Miki, who still needed light exercising and attention at least three times a week. So now they were together, and that was somewhat easier on my time.

The whole month I had been deciding about bringing in Toby, Miki seemed like he was becoming sounder. He wasn't showing any evidence of discomfort in his foot, back, or anywhere else. But we had "been there, done that" before, and I didn't trust it. Yet, my plan, which had begun with the idea of riding and training on Toby while Miki took another six months to a year to overcome all of the various maladies he had encountered, was, of necessity, changing. Miki was acting sound for four weeks straight, the longest he had gone in a year and a half. The vet and farrier team were working so well in the recovery of his lameness that he was becoming fitter and fitter as I rode him. Like a gymnast, his muscles were developing again, and because his foot wasn't in pain anymore, he was willing to work and showing very encouraging signs of athleticism. Had all of this happened a month earlier, I wouldn't have even considered uprooting Toby. I suspected his recent colic was a direct result of Toby upsetting his security.

Lord, what's happening here? I prayed in my heart.
I was reminded of the verse in Proverbs 16:2-3, *"All the
ways of a man are clean in his own sight, but the Lord
weighs the motives. Commit your works to the Lord, and
your plans will be established."* I decided I would just do
what I could do for both horses, taking it one day at a time.
God had a plan for us, and I had to see it through. After
a month of rigorous riding and training on Toby, taking
him away from Burbank and Kayla's care, hauling him to
a strange place, setting everything up, getting him on the
proper feed regimen so that he didn't drop weight, spending
extra time to help him adjust—after all that, I couldn't re-
nege now. I was committed! I began to second-guess God's
will and my prayers and then re-evaluate my motives.
Where had I gone wrong in this plan? Or, was it wrong at
all? Or, was I right where God wanted me—totally depending on Him again, which is always the best place to be!

Working with Toby brought with it many challenges. He
still was not easy for me to ride. His gaits were so big he threw
me off balance. He was strong at times and demanding that I
cue him correctly; otherwise, he didn't want to do what I was
trying to ask. He was making me learn to ask correctly! What
I began to discover as I rode Toby one day and Miki the next
was that Miki became so much easier to ride simply because
he was a bit smaller, less bouncy, and less demanding despite
his own fidgety idiosyncrasies. So what Toby was teaching
me—forcing me—to learn on his back became the training
that I needed to put Miki through his paces.

Prior to riding Toby, Miki often "had my number." He knew how to evade my cues and keep from doing the work the way I wanted him to. But now—now the tables were turned. I had *his* number! I was becoming accustomed to Toby's big size and strength so that Miki seemed like a little pony that I could just push around in the arena. Toby was training me when I didn't have the money to spend on the training I needed. I could have sworn one day that Miki turned his head around and looked me square in the eyes, and said, "Who in the world are *you*? Where's my mother, and what have you done with her?" I often chuckled over it.

Once again, God had prepared a plan for me that I

could not have envisioned. He was going to improve my riding by giving me another schoolmaster, much like Fahrenheit had been. I had bemoaned the fact that Miki's lameness for fifteen months had taken its toll on my personal equitation as well. I could not improve myself without him and indeed began to lose my timing, balance, strength, and stamina during the time off. However, every single ride on Toby's back was an accelerated lesson in something —the proper leg position, not jabbing him all the time with my spurs when he threw me off balance (he would pin his ears way back as if to say, "Get it right or I'm bucking you off!"). He forced me to keep my hands low, giving less pressure on the bit to him when he willingly went forward and gave "self-carriage" to me. He *made* me sit up straight and tall while still remaining relaxed and loose, being more precise with my aids and, above all, riding with confidence. All of this transferred over to Miki almost so effortlessly that I knew we were honing our skills together. Thanks to Toby. I realized that the Lord was using this horse to accelerate my equitation training—sort of making up for lost time!

Frank's moral support and Barbara's financial backing through all of this kept me on track. Frank always encouraged me, always listened to my personal triumphs and discouragements, and always prayed with me for "the boys" as they affectionately came to be known. Most people knew my story about Mikwaiti and the awesome gift from God he had been to me. Now I had another story about Toby. Every chance I got, I gave God the glory as I related the story of transforming BBC into Tobiah because of God's goodness to me. So, no more second-guessing. I was reminded again and again that, like Fahrenheit, Toby was my schoolmaster, so that when Miki was ready, he would be in good hands—mine—while the Lord held me in His.

CHAPTER 12

Learning to Face the Music

"For the ways of a man are before
the eyes of the LORD,
and He watches all his paths."
(Proverbs 5:21)

My time spent with the boys on a daily basis became a regular routine. Both horses were progressing nicely in their health, exercise, and training. But we had our usual bumps along the way. I was supposed to ride Miki in a Musical Kur Clinic to learn how to correctly match the musical score to the horse's tempo. It was going to be held at our ranch, which was very convenient, and I spent quite a bit of time and effort preparing for the special day.

First, I put Miki on a longe-line with side reins and trotted him from the ground in a sixty-meter circle. I had a portable metronome clipped to my watchband and timed the tick-tock of the metronome to every time Miki's inside front foot hit the ground. Having established that timing, I began to hunt for the instrumental pieces that matched it.

After that, I pulled out a video of Miki and me in a show (it was two years old, prior to his lay-up) and played the musical scores I had decided might fit. It was fun to watch our ride put to music, and before I knew it, three hours had flown by as I rewound the video over and over and played CD after CD. I had a collection of wonderful Indian CDs that I had purchased at local Powwows I enjoyed visiting. Several had great drums with a beat that I thought would fit my "Indian pony" and made notations of what sections matched the rhythm of his walk, trot, and canter. I even managed to choreograph a five-minute "dance" that included all the movements required for Second Level. I was starting to get really excited.

Well, the big day arrived, and Miki and I were due to ride at the end of the day's schedule, with six other riders before us (including a break for lunch and a lecture). I arrived at the barn at 6:30 a.m. to help set up, and the first ride was at 7:30 a.m. I was glad I had the opportunity to watch others go first because then I would know what was expected of us, and I could learn a lot by watching. Most of the riders watched each other, and there were auditors that came to observe as well. It even afforded me time to pay the barn hand an extra ten dollars to give Miki a bath. He would have plenty of time to dry.

A couple of the musicals were exhibited by two girls who had trailered up from the Pacific Palisades. They had a pair of pintos and had put together a routine for the two of them called a "pax de deux" (steps of two): "…an equestrian performance using two horses. The horses perform dressage movements, usually mirroring each other, and almost always accompanied by music" (Wikipedia). I walked up to greet them before their ride and told them I had a pinto too. They said they had seen him as they drove in and had admired him. They immediately began to discuss with me the possibility of Miki and I joining them in future exhibitions for a three-some, so that afforded me the opportunity to give them my Mikwaiti booklet since it had our picture and included my telephone number. I wondered what the future would hold for our possible three-some and their eternal destiny!

After the lunch break, the temperature got hotter and hotter. Riding at 3:30 p.m. was not going to be easy. I was beginning to feel wilted already. The ride before mine started at 2:45 p.m., so it was time for me to go start getting Miki ready. I had just enough time to dress him up nicely and allow for a fifteen-minute, light, walk-trot, warm-up ride before we entered the arena.

As I approached Miki in his paddock, he looked so beautiful. His copper coat was glistening, and his white markings were radiant. He watched me approach expectantly. I took him over to the crossties and began the routine preparation. First, as a matter of course, I would clean out the hooves and check the shoes. I picked up his infamous front left foot and stared in horror at the shoe. One of the nails had dislodged itself and bent over to the inside! How in the world did that happen in one day with him standing in his paddock on soft footing? The nail obviously hadn't stuck him in soft tissue anywhere, and it seemed secure and tight even though it was bent. I wondered if I should take a chance on riding him, even though it could possibly compromise the security of the shoe. It could come loose in the middle of the clinic and then stick him in that precious left foot!

Then I shot a glance at his front, right foot. Without even lifting it, I could see that the shoe had shifted as well—it had slid about a half-inch out of alignment. What had he done, a handstand in his stall? Obviously, he and Toby had been "playing," more like rough-housing, across their adjoining pipe. My heart sank.

At that point, I saw my friend Joy scurrying around and called her over. She confirmed my ominous feeling that I should not take a chance by riding Miki on the ill-fitting shoes. The emotion began to well up within me. All our work, all my preparation with the music and the choreography... this was the very first time since his layup for us to exhibit in public. So much for the $75 fee; that would be lost too. I was fighting back the tears.

"Go get Toby," Joy suggested. "You'll have to ride Toby."

"No! I'm not prepared with Toby. All my music is for Miki. I'm not ready with Toby!" I stammered. I knew I could ride Miki fairly well; I wasn't ready to ride Toby in front of people. He still made me feel like a novice. It would be humiliating. Plus, the rhythm of the music I had chosen for Miki wouldn't match Toby's tempo and big strides.

"At least you won't waste your entry fee," Joy dutifully reminded me. "Come on; I'll help you get ready."

She was right. I had to be responsible about the money, so I agreed and started the walk back to the paddock with Miki in tow. But I had lost precious time. If I was able to get ready in time, I had absolutely no time to warm up. And Toby took a long warm-up. He would be really fidgety and unbalanced for at least twenty minutes to a half-hour, and I only had a forty-five-minute slot. Nervousness now began to mingle with my distress and disappointment.

Lord, why? I was so looking forward to this! Why did this have to happen? All the fun was gone and replaced with dread. The joy of showing how well Miki and I were doing was about to be replaced with disillusionment and embarrassment.

I pulled Toby out with an affectionate pat on the neck. He was going to become Miki's replacement once again. *At least Miki isn't hurt this time*; I comforted myself with the thought. But Toby was filthy. Of all days, he looked like he had spent the night in a pig pen rolling around in the slop! *Oh, Toby,* I groaned. Out of time or not, he *had* to be rinsed!

In less than twenty minutes, I managed to totally rinse him off, get his leg wraps on (I didn't even have the typical white ones used to dress up a dressage horse, but had to use my well-worn practice pair). With Joy's and Frank's help, I got him saddled and bridled and got my own outfit and polished boots on. I hopped into the saddle, and we strolled down to the dressage arena.

The clinician did the best she could with using music selected for Miki. I didn't even have the presence of mind to tell her what happened and that we should scratch the music I had prepared for Miki. But we discovered that the beat of the music to Miki's trot fit Toby's canter instead. She eventually found some other pieces in her repertoire that complimented Toby's way of going. But he wasn't easy on me at first and, as expected, didn't really settle into what we were doing for at least ten minutes. But he did settle in sooner than I expected, and I was grateful to him. He seemed to know I needed him to be kind to me. Who knows, maybe the music relaxed him.

After about a half-hour performing in the arena, with the temperatures soaring and my droopy state of mind, I thought I might just expire right there in front of every-body! And we were being videotaped. Had anyone ever fainted on camera? I could have been the first. But I knew that Toby and I had had some good moments together, and I was grateful for that and so grateful, once again, for his effort. The heat and the unusual surroundings were not easy on him either. After all, he walked into the arena he was accustomed to by that time, only to be visually assaulted by a big red tarp set up on the side for shade. There were lots of white chairs all around, with people moving and talking, not to mention music blaring out of a boom box! And, let's face it, in the heat, he did most of the work. Yes, riding takes strength and energy, but my mental attitude struggled more than my physical state. I could only imagine how Toby felt running around for almost an hour in the heat with 130 pounds on his back. It made me appreciate Tobiah's willingness even more. The "goodness of God" was, once again, my hero.

Besides all that, I was getting tired. Having a horse is a lot of work. Having two horses caused me to have to really streamline my schedule! Again, I began to second-guess what I had done. Had I pursued my will thinking it was God's? Is God's will always the smoothest road? My Christian experience reminded me that was not the case. I had been on bumpy roads and seemingly dead ends before, and God always illuminated the path at the right time. I knew that God doesn't promise us "happy trails" all the time, but He does promise to ride alongside and be our Divine scout, as the Scripture says,

> *The steps of a man are established by the Lord; and He delights in his way. When he falls, he will not be hurled headlong; because the Lord is the one who holds his hand* (Psalm 37:23-24).

My schedule would have been easier without Toby, but I would have missed out on God's intended benefit.

Lessons from the Sparrow

Several months later, by the middle of the summer, however, it became excruciatingly apparent that I could not keep Toby because expenses had increased. I had ridden him for four months and had just made a breakthrough with him, feeling in tune with his movements and secure in the saddle. But now, he had a medical issue, and I couldn't afford the extra food and care. He had developed an imbalance in his left hind leg due to a newly diagnosed muscle weakness. Big horses like him need extra protein to build their muscles, much like bodybuilders in the gym. Also, he was unable to assimilate carbohydrates for energy or muscle development. The deficiency was in his bloodline. By the time Barbara had discovered it in his half-sister, he was already in my care, and we scrambled to adjust his diet for the protein and fat that was needed to keep him strong. Thankfully, however, Miki had remained consistently sound, and I felt the pressure to provide him with the training that he needed—that I had always wanted for him. We couldn't afford to keep both horses healthy and sound the way they both deserved. We began to discuss and pray about alternatives.

The timing was such that Frank and I had just moved

to another part of the valley, which put me an *additional* twelve miles further away from the boys. The time spent in the round-trip commutes was also becoming an added burden in Southern California traffic. I had seen another ranch near our house in Saugus owned and managed by a wonderful couple, Jim and Connie, who also rode and ran a training program as well. We decided to pay a visit on a quiet Sunday afternoon. We were warmly greeted and found the accommodations much to our liking. The prices were a little higher for one horse, but after being accustomed to providing for two, the cost became doable. I was excited about the nice in-and-out box stall Miki would enjoy, while at the same time, my heart began to softly grieve over the prospect of losing Toby. I had become much attached to him, wasn't intimidated by him any longer, finally felt confident in the saddle, and actually rode him well! Sensing God's leading and timing, we prayed for Toby that the Lord would care for him in a special way and provide a healthy and happy environment for him to live in. With that prayer under my belt, I garnered the courage to call Barbara and tell her of our difficult decision. Undaunted, not only did Barbara understand, but she was already armed with a recommendation of someone she knew who was looking for a horse to adopt. She gave me the number of an old, mutual acquaintance named Diane.

Diane's equestrian escapades had landed her a third place in the Prix St. George test at the Volvo World Cup in 1996 on her gorgeous Thoroughbred gelding, Chauncey.

But a serious automobile accident soon thereafter had cut short her dreams for advancing to the Olympics by breaking her neck and placing her in a long and difficult two-year recuperation. But recuperate, she did, and she wanted a horse she could ride for the sheer pleasure of it and share with her husband without the physical stresses of personally training and showing Chauncey any longer.

It was a beautiful Saturday morning in mid-August, just before the heat of the day, when Diane and her husband, John, made the long trip from Simi Valley to Santa Clarita to meet Toby and watch him go through his paces. I had him spit-shined and polished and climbed onto his huge back for an exhibition ride. I needed them to like him! But there was an adjustment period for his new medicinal diet, and he was right in the middle of that recuperation. I held my breath as I started Toby off in the warm-up trot. I was hoping it wouldn't be obvious that day, but it was. In fact, it seemed exaggerated. Sometimes he warmed up better in the right lead canter, since it is only a three-beat gait rather than the four-beat of the trot, and took some pressure off the left hind leg. But his canter was off—way off. *Oh no, Lord,* I groaned deep inside. *No one will want to take a lame horse. Please help us!*

I just decided to discuss the obvious. Toby and I stood in front of Diane and John while I explained in detail his struggle with the muscle deterioration, the new diet he was on, the symptoms they were observing, and the good prognosis after a few more months of regulating his diet and exercise. All Diane could say was how beautiful he was!

We all decided the best thing to do was just let her mount up. She straddled his tall frame and began to walk the arena, cueing him to certain movements in the walk. He was responsive to her kind hands and gentle aids, and they seemed to enjoy their first encounter with each other. By the time we took off his tack, cleaned him up, and put him away with his treats, Diane and John had made their decision to take him. I was floored and grateful! Diane and I hugged—I cried tears of joy mixed with sadness; she cried tears of joy.

I arranged to move Toby the following weekend, so, with the help of my friend, Patty, we got the trailer hooked up and ready to go. I hoped Toby would load without any trouble; he was too big a horse to fight with! But Barbara had trained him well. He obediently walked on, following me up to the hay bag, where he immediately began to forage the alfalfa sticking through the twine. I closed up the ramp, and we were off.

Taking him to the rancho area of Simi Valley was an adventure, mainly because neither Patty nor I had been there before, and we were amazed at seeing a planned bedroom community replete with bridle paths, several association arenas, and mountain trails around homes that had pastures and barn facilities behind their well-manicured back yards. It was lovely. It was an equestrian's planned-neighborhood paradise.

We unloaded Toby at his new home—a large box stall with featherbed shavings attached to an outside paddock that was as big as what I had him in at home. It had a view of the entire Simi Valley. My heart overflowed with peace and excitement at the same time. I couldn't have imagined anything nicer for him, and my guilty feelings of abandoning him were quickly wiped away. He was going to be much better off. And Diane and John were enamored with him and had the means to keep him vetted and sound. He would be truly loved. They would even keep his name as Toby!

Patty and I floated home, it seemed. She chattered like a chipmunk in her enthusiasm about Toby's good fortune, which kept my emotions in check. It wasn't until about three days later that I began to really struggle with his absence at the barn. I felt a pang of grief and loss. But Miki didn't! As bonded as they had finally become, the minute I opened the gate between their two paddocks, Miki walked through it, over to Toby's abandoned food trough, and began to eat. I had been praying for him too, hoping the removal of his stall-buddy would not be as traumatic as was his arrival (causing the colic). He seemed to say, "Toby was a nice companion, but I'm glad to have my old stall back, thank you very much!" His adjustment was immediate and uneventful. I couldn't have asked for more.

But more I got. After about two weeks, I called Diane

to see how she and Toby were getting along. She said he was already spoiled—new blankets, new saddle, new bridle, and, best of all, gaining weight. She invited me out to see. I took her up on her offer and drove out on a Saturday afternoon. Sure enough, Toby looked great and toyed with remembering my familiar neck-scratching on his favorite "spot." But I could see the affection being showered on him by Diane and John.

I helped saddle him up, and Diane rode him a couple of blocks down the bridle path "sidewalk" to the arena. John and I followed in his car. In the arena, we were met by the gal who rode Chauncey for Diane in a weekly lesson. Diane decided she could teach the lesson more easily from the ground and offered Toby's back to me. I didn't hesitate. It was a strange familiarity: the bigness, the long neck, the big strides as we walked the arena. Before long, Diane invited us into the training session, and there we were, Toby and I, back together again—even getting a lesson. In fact, Diane invited me to ride him as often as I liked. Only the driving distance prevented me from making it daily again. But we did manage a weekly ride for several weeks until Miki's show schedule began to take precedence.

This season of riding Toby in his beautiful new surroundings helped to wean me emotionally from him. I hadn't lost him after all and didn't really have to give him up totally. God, in His "goodness," had returned all of it back to me—which seems to be His pattern in my life.

My God is a generous God of grace and mercy. That truth should never be underestimated or forgotten. And at times like these, when the Creator God is mindful of the welfare of His dependent creatures, even the four-footed kind, my heart wells up with thanksgiving and praise. For He is the God who is mindful of every hop of the sparrow *"And not one of them falls to the ground apart from your Father's will"* (Matthew 10:29b, NKJV). Surely, He can house a homeless horse like Toby, give peace in the potentially disorienting situation Miki was in, and bring comfort to a frail human caretaker such as myself, who often finds the stewardship of such magnificent gifts overwhelming.

I needed my focus to be on God's will for Miki, his training, and his showing. And at the Saugus barn, under the watchful eye of my new coach, Julie, God was working together incredible details to prepare us for the show circuit. Our first show in three years was already scheduled. I had recently read a devotional from one of my favorite preachers from the 1800s, Charles Haddon Spurgeon. It was especially poignant:

> Your wants were innumerable, and therefore the supplies have been infinitely great, and your prayers have been as varied as the mercies have been countless. Then have you not cause to say, "I love the Lord, because He hath heard the voice of my supplication?" For as your prayers have been many, so also have been God's answers to

them. He has heard you in the day of trouble, has strengthened you, and helped you, even when you dishonored Him by trembling and doubting at the mercy seat. Remember this, and let it fill your heart with gratitude to God, who has thus graciously heard your poor weak prayers. "Bless the Lord, O my soul, and forget not all His benefits."[xi]

CHAPTER 13

Death of a Vision

~~

Birth of Another

"Behold, I say to you, lift up your eyes
and look at the fields,
for they are already white for harvest!"
(John 4:35, NKJV)

As time went on, Miki greatly improved, and we began the show circuit again, which became my priority. It was a year of promise, the year I had been waiting for! Miki wasn't lame anymore, and the new season was just beginning. There were many memberships to renew in associations that provided various benefits to the competitors, so it was important to show in four-star or at least triple-rated shows.

First, there was the American Horse Show Association (AHSA). They are the umbrella organization over all aspects of equine competition, whether Western or English. They offered oversight of rules and regulations for all equestrian sports along with special insurance coverage for competitors.

Then, there was the United States Dressage Federation (USDF). This functioned in similar fashion to the AHSA, but more specifically to the sport of dressage, and offered special recognition and awards to contenders.

The Dressage Association of Southern California (DASC) was formed as a spin-off from the California Dressage Society (CDS—see below) and was one single club offering local clinics, championships, and prizes to its members.

Lastly, CDS was broken down into chapters, and I belonged to the Santa Clarita Valley Chapter (SCV), as mentioned earlier. The CDS-SCV offered more localized schooling shows, clinics, and educational programs with accompanying awards and prizes within the local chapters. I had the privilege of being one of the founding officers of the Santa Clarita Chapter and served in that capacity for three years, reaping much personal satisfaction and friendships.

For the upper levels, even Olympic level riders, the Federation Equestre Internationale (FEI) functioned. The FEI World Equestrian Games are the major international championships for equestrianism and are administered by the FEI. The games have been held every four years, halfway between the sets of consecutive Summer Olympic Games, since 1990. Of course, this was way out of my league, but records were still maintained by them.

I joined and paid the membership fees wherever required. By this time, Miki and I had moved to another barn closer to home, where his training became more consistent. A wonderful trainer I met, Maggie Broekman, did more for us in our many months together than we had been able to accomplish prior to that. The consistency, of course, made the difference. But the training technique was so focused that I was able to concentrate on the constant, moment-by-moment, stride-by-stride instructions. My body went into automatic gear, responding without struggle to what my ears were hearing and my mind was comprehending. I saw great progress being made in my equitation and, as a result, in Miki's understanding of my aids.

Practicing the canter and trot in a double bridle.

I remember hearing Robert Dover (another of the team of four Olympic Bronze Medalists in Dressage Team 1996, Atlanta) say at one of his clinics I attended that "No matter what the horse does, right or wrong, make sure that what you are doing is right!" I began to see the fruit of that statement under expert tutelage, as she focused primarily on what my seat, hands, and legs were correctly feeling and doing, rather than just on how Miki was looking. One, of course, led to the other, and I learned that a championship ride consisted more often with the expertise of the rider (80 percent) than to the athleticism of the horse (20 percent). In other words, if a poorly trained rider rode a million-dollar dressage horse, that horse would not perform for what it was worth.

So, I began to enter show after show, attempting to collect my scores and certificates in First Level for that show season to make up for the lost time in order to be able to move up to Second Level the following year. Miki and I were a real team. It was often that we would have to go alone without Frank, or our trainer, or another show team. We went to the Southern California shows closest to us, which were plentiful—at least every other weekend. I became comfortably accustomed to preparing the trailer with bedding, alfalfa hay, and water, plus packing all of Miki's tack and grooming equipment in the dressing room, along with my own show clothes. Plus, I had to bathe the horse and braid his mane. It was a lot of work, and I ran on pure enthusiasm.

Miki had shipping boots that he wore to protect his legs and feet from accidentally stepping on himself and causing injury. Every time I brought them out and plopped the container on the ground outside his stall, his ears would perk, and he would back away into a corner of his stall. He knew what was coming... he was going somewhere! He also had a shipping halter, leather-covered with sheep skin to prevent rubbing, which would be softer on his head in case he braced against it in transport. Once he was all "dressed" and ready to go, I put a stud chain on his lead and allowed it to rest underneath his muzzle. It was there as a reminder that he was to go where I led him and in no other direction. With horse in my right hand and a long dressage whip in my left in case I needed to tap him forward, we would walk to the gaping mouth of the trailer's double doors opened and awaiting its passenger.

Miki was used to this routine because periodically, we also had to trailer out to meet up with his farrier if he was unable to come to us that week. I became an expert at loading, hauling, parking, and maneuvering truck and trailer in and out of tight spots. The part Miki liked the best was the alfalfa hay. His daily stall food was grass hay because the alfalfa was so rich in protein that it caused him to urinate too much. Horses eat grass; cows eat alfalfa (many European experts would say). But he loved the alfalfa! So, I would often let him peek in the side window of his trailer just to see and sniff the alfalfa that was there waiting for him. Within minutes he would practically load himself. Of course, he always received a sugar lump or two once he was in his trailer stall and hooked up, ready to roll.

It was important to get to the show grounds early, so, depending upon how far we had to go or what time our particular class was, we often left quite early on Saturday mornings (I wouldn't show on Sundays because I saved those days for church with Frank). Once on the grounds, I needed to leave Miki alone in his trailer while I checked in. He didn't like that part and would stomp his feet when the trailer stopped, saying, "Let me out!" But I would open his window and let him stick his big beautiful head out to look around and keep his eye on me as best he could. When the time was right, all I had to do was open the rear doors, walk inside to unhook his halter from the manger area, connect the lead to his halter, and allow him to back out while I held onto his lead. I didn't have a ramp but had a step-down, which he maneuvered carefully in reverse. We both became so used to this that I was able to unhook him through his window, throw the lead over his back, and allow him to back out on his own as I grabbed hold of the lead on the outside.

There was a tie bar on the side of the trailer where I could loosely tie him while I began to tack him up for the show. There can be lots of commotion at the show grounds with other contenders doing what I was doing, other mounted riders going by, tractors roaring as they leveled arenas that had been well-used already. Miki became "seasoned" to all of that, and I was so proud of him. He was a true show horse.

Horses' temperaments can change at a show as well. They can become either hyper-sensitive or dulled down in order to mentally handle the sensory overload. Miki sometimes would go both ways. I remember more than one show; after an uneventful warm-up time of about fifteen minutes, we entered the arena, and I felt like he had the brakes on. I couldn't get him to perform with any pizzazz or fire in his belly... we just did the routine, and I felt exhausted afterward from trying to urge him onward. Those were definitely not blue-ribbon rides. Then there were times, more often than not, that he was so hyper-minded that the slightest movement I made, weight change, aids with my fingers slightly signaling the reins, or my calves lightly on his belly, he was *there* for me—forward, on the bit, his beautiful neck rounded, *almost* feeling out of control, but not. A little nerve-wracking for me, but those were the winning rides! Of course, it was all mental attitude. When he was forward and animated, it meant that he was feeling over-stimulated by our environment. It was always a delicate balance to keep his attention on me so that he would do what I asked.

We even put together and showed a First Level Musical Freestyle. The first time we performed it, we were the exhibition at a schooling show for other riders. That was an honor for us because everyone stopped what they were doing and gathered around our arena to watch.

Miki was like a bolt of lightning—brilliant—and way

more hyper than I wanted him to be. But he had a way of going that brought admiration and applause, not to mention he was just beautiful under saddle. The judge of the schooling show made the comment, "Boy, can he sit!" That meant that he was using his hind end and giving the appearance of traveling uphill. A horse that can sit well can perform the upper-level movements of piaffe or passage more easily. Miki was a natural, but I had difficulty getting him to do it because I had not been trained how to ask for it. However, he showed it to me several times out on trail if something scared him. Then he scared me!

After that, I was ready to apply at a triple-rated show to do our musical. It was a bit more complicated because I had to bring my music and get it set up in a boom box on the side. My friend, Kris, came with me to help with that part. But Miki was just so distracted by all that was going on, he sidestepped off course where he should not have and refused to go forward in another part of the pattern. It was disappointing, to say the least, and I felt a little humiliated since a lot of people like to stop and watch when they hear the music playing. We finally left the arena after our futile attempt, and there was Hilda Gurney sitting off by the side. To my chagrin, she gave me what encouragement she could with the comment, "I really liked your music."

It is typical practice to school beyond the level being shown, so we were schooling some of the more challenging patterns and movements in Third Level to prepare for the

Second Level show season. Miki was talented and doing well, but there was a glitch. After months of training, showing at triple-rated shows, hauling Miki all over Southern California by myself to get to the various venues, making sure that my membership was intact, and showing my card to all of the show staff everywhere I went, I found out at the end of the year that *none* of my scores counted! Evidently, I had a General Membership to the United States Dressage Federation (USDF) rather than an Individual Membership. None of the show staff remarked about it at the time, assuming, I'm sure, that I knew what I was doing. Since I was traveling alone through the show circuit, I didn't have a trainer with me to make sure all the "t's" were crossed and the "i's" dotted. It was totally devastating and demoralizing, not to mention the time and expense spent in the effort for equipment, training, gas, and show fees. I would have to acquire my First Level scores all over again before being allowed to advance to Second Level.

Frank and I had to have one of "those talks" about the budget, and it became obvious that the previous year's shows at First Level could not be re-done. The expenses had to be cut back. I complied and was grateful that at least I still had my sweet boy, Miki. I thought back on Miki's performances, after all the struggles and bouts of lameness, and was so proud of him! Our escapades together were numerous: some tense, some funny, some exhausting.

A Tumbling Tumbleweed

So, back on the trails we went. One of my new riding buddies, Sharon, and I decided to take a long ride on a Saturday morning. We had to walk our horses along some of the paved streets of the neighborhood in order to get to the rugged California hills where the trails began. It was a beautiful day and a pleasant beginning. The horses behaved well on the asphalt, and the minimal traffic was respectful not to get too close.

We had to cross a grassy lot to get to the trail head, which began a steady incline and outlined part of a golf course on one side. It was a pretty area, but the footing on the trail (which was really a fire-access road going up into the hills) was packed hard with a few ruts along the way up and down the other side. The horses carefully maneuvered the ruts, taking wide steps to cross over. We walked up for about twenty minutes, rode around the ridge for a while, and decided it was time to head back. The horses were very alert while in this wilderness area but remained calm and obedient to our cues.

Once we reached the fire road which led to home, there was another slight incline to cross over the hilltop and start back down the other side. As a matter of course, it is always wise to walk a horse when headed for home base—they have a keen sense of direction and can get overly excited when they know they are approaching home—and food! So, we decided to just walk, single file, with Sharon's mare in front. I had Miki on a loose rein so that he could relax his neck as he began the climb. Suddenly, Sharon's horse started to canter, and she belted out, "Well, I guess she decided to run!" instead of reigning her in. That, of course, caught Miki and I both completely by surprise. Not wanting to be left behind, Miki bolted forward with a lurch since we were starting uphill, and I let out a little yell of shock. His bolt caused me to go off balance slightly, but I quickly began to gather up the reins to halt him. At the very next stride, however, he had to jump over one of those ruts that suddenly appeared before him in the road and, at a run, he obviously couldn't negotiate it any other way. Already being off balance slightly, I could not recover from the jump and felt myself slipping. To my detriment, along came another rut in the road, and Miki's next jump sent me flying off the back of the saddle. Since we were headed on an upward incline, the distance down Miki's backside was longer than normal as I landed downhill, hard on my back on the concrete-hard dirt, with a thud and an "oomph," forcing all the air in my lungs out of my mouth. All of this, from the first lurch to the final jump, took about five seconds, from which there was no recovery! Now I was hurt—and badly!

Sharon swung her mare around and rode back to me. "Are you alright!?" she asked. "What can I do?" "G-g-go g-g-get Miki," I groaned. I couldn't catch my breath and couldn't move. Sharon swung around again and headed up the trail to try to find Miki. Thankfully, he had come to a stop up ahead, certainly wondering where I had gone! She grabbed his reins and brought him down to me. Somehow I had to get up. All I could do was slowly turn onto my side and slowly, very slowly get to my hands and knees, grab the side fence and pull myself up. But we were a long way from the ranch, and there was no way I could walk. I had to get back on Miki, but how?

He stood perfectly still as I climbed the bottom rail of the three-railed fence so that I could manage to put my foot in the stirrup and gingerly swing the other leg over the saddle. I honestly don't know how I managed to do it, but I did. I just wanted to get back to the barn because I was in serious pain. We had to walk the horses *very* slowly because just the rhythmic movement of Miki's back was almost more than I could bear. I called ahead, notifying my friend, Vicki, that I had fallen off Miki's back and to be prepared to meet us when we got there. Thirty agonizing minutes later, we arrived, and Vicki took Miki off my hands, kindly cleaned him up, and put him away. By that time, I was feeling numb and must have been in shock (or denial) because Vicki and I and a couple of others went out to lunch afterward! I never did go to the doctor, and should have, because it took me weeks to heal from the agonizing pain of what I assumed was just bruised ribs.

A year or two later, my injury came back to haunt me, literally. I had had an ultra sound for another more benign reason, and the doctors noticed a "spot" on my kidney, suggesting it could be cancer and recommended further tests.

That petrified me—I beseeched the Lord in prayer at every thought of it. It was during this agonizing waiting period of several weeks that I memorized all sixteen verses of Psalm 91, which was of great comfort to me. These verses below were especially poignant:

> *Surely He shall deliver you...from the perilous pestilence. His truth shall be your shield and buckler. No evil shall befall you, Nor shall any plague come near your dwelling; For He shall give His angels charge over you, To keep you in all your ways* (Psalm 91:3-4, 9-10, NKJV).

My mind and heart continually sought the refuge of the Lord. I was trusting Him to "deliver" me from the "perilous pestilence." Truly, "His truth" became my protective shield. After weeks of waiting, a final test was scheduled at UCLA with, I was told, "the finest and best kidney doctor" on the west coast. He looked at my ultra sound, X-rays, etc., and summarily dismissed me with a nonchalant comment, "I've seen so many test results that look threatening, but yours isn't one of them." Evidently, the fall-off Miki onto my back while we were on trail, had caused trauma to that kidney, and what they were seeing by ultrasound was a scar, not a growth! The doctor said, "Go home and enjoy your life," or something to that effect. I was in a mental fog, but that's exactly what I did! I began to share with all my friends the wonderful news I had received. What if the doctor's prognosis had been different? I began to openly share the good news of what God had done for me in answering my prayer for His protection from kidney cancer.

Miki's Missionary Journey

Through the many years of enjoying this beautiful animal, it became very apparent to me that we had a different—a better—an eternal purpose. We had stayed several years at various Santa Clarita ranches and solidified several friendships that lasted through many years. My commitment to my faith in Christ was always my priority, however. That usually resulted in opportunities to pass out my *Mikwaiti* booklet in order to share the gospel. Most people were very receptive to receiving it because we all shared an interest in each other's horses, and no one else that I had met had written down their "story" like I did, which ignited their curiosity. My friend, Katie, who had helped me when Miki had colic, expressed an interest in spiritual things, and after a while, Frank and I began to meet at her house to study the Bible together. We did so for a couple of years and shared rich fellowship even while on many trail rides together.

Periodically, as I moved Miki to a different ranch for one reason or another, it became clear to me that the moves were directed by the Lord, even though I might have thought at the time that sometimes unpleasant circumstances were regretful; however, there would be somebody at the new place that either needed encouragement or was curious about what it meant to be a Christian. Frank even went so far as to purchase a license plate holder for my horse trailer that said: "Miki's Missionary Journey." There were a couple of occasions when someone would tell me that they felt *they* were the reason I had moved there—just to be able to speak with them about Christ! One particular gentleman was an Egyptian from the Middle East and not at all interested in what I had to say, even mockingly nicknaming me "Joan of Arc." However, before he moved to a different barn, we were able to have a meaningful talk about my Christian faith, and he gladly, finally, received Mikwaiti's booklet. God's Word goes forth to where it is intended, and who knows what past relationships I will meet up with in heaven someday!

Equestrienne Bible Study

I found that as various friends from the different ranches responded positively to my message and outreach with Miki, I felt the burden to teach them more solid spiritual "food." Since they were all so spread out from ranch to ranch, I was unable to get them to come to my church in the Valley. So, we began a ladies' Bible study in my home once a week. We studied the "Fundamentals of the Faith" by John MacArthur for a number of years together in order to give them a solid and unified understanding of God and the Bible. From there, we started to dig into a book of the

Bible, specifically the epistle of the apostle Paul to the Philippians and had a rich time of teaching, conversation, and even a few conversions. It was a rich nine years together, and we all became very close.

Loretta, Susan, Karen, Karen, Deb, me, Bev, Lisa, Lorri, Kelli, Peggy

CHAPTER 14

When Change Comes

"By faith Abraham, when he was called,
obeyed by going out to a place which he was to
receive for an inheritance;
and he went out, not knowing where he was going."
(Hebrews 11:8)

Miki and I enjoyed many more years of arena riding, practicing what we had learned during our show years, and going out on "trail" rides around the neighborhoods of the different barns where he lived. Finally, in July of 2013, Miki and I celebrated two more blue-ribbon rides in California in the newly emerging sport of Western Dressage! We weren't involved in the show season any longer, but Western Dressage was so new that all I had to do was apply for a slot without joining any of the typical dressage clubs. The Western trainer at my current barn encouraged us to try. She knew we would do well because of all our years in the English riding sport. So, I agreed, and she slapped her beautiful leather and silver Western saddle on Miki so we could practice. Of course, in a totally different kind of saddle, it not only felt very odd to him but also to me. My seat was different and had less contact with his back—the Western saddle was thick, so I had to communicate more by shifting my weight, and my legs touched him with more effort, being placed more forward on his torso than we were accustomed to. The English saddle we had been using for years seemed like a postage stamp by comparison. Plus, the Western saddle was much heavier, especially with all the silver trim. I wasn't even sure how to cinch it up properly. Nevertheless, we had three months to practice, and we both got used to it. Miki continually amazed me the way he would just take things "in stride" (pun intended). He was at the healthy but ripe age of twenty-three, still athletic, willing, and responding to the feeling of the new saddle beautifully. It caused me to reminisce about riding his father, Modern Creation, when he was that age and just as willing to try something new.

Thankfully, for the Western dressage test, we were still able to use the English direct rein, which has tension between the rider's hands and the horse's mouth literally directing his head in the direction the horse is supposed to go. Neck reining used in Western riding is where the horse responds to light pressure of the rein against its neck on one side, instructing the horse to turn to the opposite side and vice versa.

We competed in two classes: First Level Test One and Test Two. After winning both tests, Miki was the "star" of the ranch for a while.

Horses can be considered "seniors" at around eighteen and are often retired from the show ring earlier than that. I knew this show was our "last hurrah," and God was so gracious to allow us to walk away once and for all from the show world with our heads held high as we looked up to Him in praise!

But another change was right around the corner. After twenty years of my unusual equestrian ministry, unexpected circumstances caused Frank and me to have to consider moving. We had both been forced to retire, so our income was cut in half. Leaving our home, all our beloved friends at church, and my friends at the various barns, especially the Equestrienne Bible Study gals, was extremely disheartening and sad. Reluctantly leaving tore at the very fabric of our hearts.

My sister, Carol, lived near Charlottesville in Central

Virginia, where she and her husband, Jim, indicated that rent and cost of living were cheaper. We decided to pay a visit, especially after having dinner one night with friends, Jim and Charlotte, explaining our dilemma of having to move. When we mentioned Virginia, Jim shouted, "Virginia! I love Virginia!" Jim was also a horse lover and talked about the annual pre-Christmas parade in a little town in the north called Middleburg, an authentic Colonial town steeped in history just outside the nation's capital. Usually held around the second week of December, a fox-hunt club strolled their horses down Main Street with all of their hunt hounds.

Charlotte's sister lived there, and they had visited a year or two earlier. He challenged us to look up the Middleburg Parade on the computer, which we did the minute we got home. That was all it took! There was a photo of a hunt club with all their red jackets and spotted hounds around the horses' legs, with light snow falling around them!

Omigosh! How romantic, we thought! That was September of 2014, and we made plane reservations to arrive for the parade festivities by the second week of December. Jim promised to pay special attention to Miki while we were on our trip. He was a tall man and made Miki appear small! But he had grown quite attached to him through our friendship and had even ridden him once. Miki was comfortable being with him.

Our plane landed early on the Saturday of the parade,

and we drove a rental car to Middleburg to catch their shuttle to the parade route on Main Street. The drive was so beautiful, and we rejoiced at being there for the occasion and seeing the gorgeous, sprawling, green farms (green being a color we did not see much of in Southern California). As we drove, sensing God's grace to us, our favorite song, "Overwhelmed," performed by Big Daddy Weave, came on the Christian radio station we found:

> I see the work of Your hands... I delight myself in You, captivated by Your beauty,
> Oh, God, I'm overwhelmed by You... all that You've done is so overwhelming.
> You are beautiful, you are wonderful, You are glorious,
> Oh God, there is no one more glorious, You are the most glorious.
> I delight myself in You, in the glory of Your presence.
> ... I run into Your arms, unashamed because of mercy.
> There is no one more beautiful![xii]

It had been raining lightly, but we sang along with enthusiasm. We parked the car on the grassy lot provided and took the shuttle to town with a half-hour to spare. Then I discovered that my brand-new iPhone was missing! So, we prayed together and got back on the shuttle to return to the car to find it. I crawled around on the first shuttle that

had dropped us off, looking under the seats, while Frank
went to check in the car. I found nothing, and neither did he
until the Lord directed him at the last minute to look down
outside our car after he had locked it up and was ready to
leave. There it was, safely laying in the grass! Frank was
so excited that he began to run across the field in the rain
toward the shuttle I was in, waving the phone in the air.
He tripped and did a face-plant right into the muddy grass,
arms outstretched, and the newly found phone went right
into the mud with him. He finally appeared at the door of
the shuttle with a big white toothy grin at his discovery,
outlined by all the mud on his front—unhurt but happy! My
phone cleaned up just fine... Frank took a little more effort
to spruce up. Then back on the shuttle, we went back to
town, thanking the Lord that our excitement had not been
dampened, at least figuratively.

Middleburg was by no means a let-down, except there
was no fun snow yet, even though it was chilly from the
sprinkle of winter rain. But that didn't dampen our spirits
either. The little town was quaint, the Colonial storefronts
and hotels beautifully decorated with festive wreathes and
Christmas bobbles. We had been invited by Charlotte's sister, Vikki, and her husband Charlie, for lunch in their dar-
ling cottage nearby, along with another young couple, Tom
and Alley. Charlie prayed a beautiful prayer over the food
as we all held hands. I learned that young Tom and Alley
were not believers, so I was able to give them Mikwaiti's
gospel booklet, which probably made me happier than it did

them at the time. Then the six of us went out to watch the parade together. It was cold…to thin-blooded Frank and me!

Virginia! ...Here We Come...

We had found a new enthusiasm in the midst of the heartache of leaving California. I pondered another favorite verse from Isaiah 65:24 (KJV): *"Before they call, I will answer; while they are still speaking, I will hear."* God had prepared the way before us and was with us each step, so we were pretty much sold on the idea of moving to Virginia, yet we needed to know where we could live with our menagerie of pets. It was a joy to reunite finally with sister Carol and husband Jim, whom we hadn't seen since the sad reunion at our parents' funerals over twenty years earlier.

They committed to helping with moving in, organizing, decorating, and shopping, and we spent the week driving all around the countryside near Charlottesville looking for a place to rent and the possibility of a farm for Miki. He was my main concern since the rest of us would easily adapt by just being together. But the change for Miki would be more drastic. We made plans to arrive sometime in the early spring, which the local real estate agent we retained (a horse gal—wouldn't you know) said was the optimum time to find open rentals. We began to experience a bit of culture shock, especially with the cold December weather, the driving distances, not knowing where we were most of the time, and finding it difficult to plan how to get family, house, job, and horse all within proximity of one another. However, once we were back home, we had plenty of time to prepare, and we kept in touch with our agent, who sent virtual tours or pictures of possible homes to rent. We were able to sell our house in one day for cash at the asking price with a sixty-day escrow, which gave us time to pack and plan. We really felt God's Hand on our plans as we laid them out before Him continually.

We finally moved, lock, stock, and barrel. The "stock" included three dogs, a cat, and eventually Miki. From February 27 to March 3, 2015, Frank and I trekked the five-night, six-day, 2700-mile drive in our truck and horse trailer, loaded with four animals, all their food and bedding, and some household items that we hadn't shipped beforehand—minus the horse—almost like "The Beverly Hillbillies" in reverse. Hauling Miki would have been too much responsibility for us and too traumatic for him, so I left him in Barbara's capable and caring hands while we got to our new home site and got settled in. It was difficult saying goodbye to him, knowing we would be apart for several months. That was early February.

We sensed the Lord's protection over us the entire way, starting with our decision to leave on a Thursday instead of waiting until the planned-for Saturday departure. Our house was emptied, and we were just sleeping on the floor. We had been able to shorten the escrow and didn't want to wait until spring, so why wait another day?

I secured the back seat of our Chevy Tahoe with harnesses for the two big dogs, Toni and Bennett, so they would be as safe during transport as possible. I put fifteen lb. Sugar, a Maltipoo, into a crate that was belted down so she wouldn't get crushed under the weight of the two fifty lb. Portuguese Water Dogs. Pinto, the cat, had the seat of honor—the entire boot of the Tahoe filled with his crate, which housed his Buda Box filled with litter, his food bowl, and a soft zip-lined carrier that he could lay in to feel sheltered and safe.

I honestly thought the cat would be the most traumatized and cause us trouble during the trip, but of course, as cats like to do, he proved me wrong.

We made our first trek to Tucson, Arizona, in nine hours, traveling just ahead of a big rain storm that hit Southern California the next day. Had we waited until Saturday, we would have had treacherous travel along the crowded California freeways hauling a horse trailer in a wild rainstorm where, when it rains, it pours. We were dog-tired our first day, and so were the dogs. We realized that nine hours would be about the maximum drive time we could handle in a given day.

Nevertheless, the dogs were on the adventure of their lives with happy, panting smiles and wagging tails, delighted to get into the car, or out of the car, and back into the car. They loved every gas stop we made, sniffing every new smell.

They gleefully joined us in the "pet rooms" of the hotels where we stayed. We were quite the attraction, filling the hotel cart with our suitcase, coats, a barrel of dog food, dog beds, and a cat in a carrier while attempting to control three excited dogs on leashes. I knew that all my years of hauling Miki around from pillar to post with all his paraphernalia had prepared me for such a time as this. We got more than a few stares, however, and a lot of smiles.

Because it was still wintertime, there were weather reports from all over the country. The shipping company that was going to bring Miki at a later time recommended that we take the southern route across the continent, which we did. We had our route all planned out and had reservations for where we would stay each night. But when we finally got to Texas by the third night, they had freezing rain, which closed down the route between Van Horn and Odessa. We had pulled into the only gas station in that tiny little town to gas up before we went over the grade to head north, and I got out to go to the restroom. When I came out, Frank met me at the door wide-eyed, notifying me that the pass was impassable! He was told by other drivers who pulled up with snow piled on their hoods that it was icing over and cars were getting stranded off the side of the road. While he continued on to the restroom, I spotted a police car at a gas pump! Have I ever in my life seen a police car at a gas pump? No! Thank You, Lord! So I walked over to one of the officers and asked if he thought we should attempt to make the drive over the pass.

He asked, "Is that your rig?" nodding towards our horse trailer hooked up to the Tahoe.

"Yes," I said.

"Then I wouldn't advise it. If your trailer starts to slide sideways behind you, it will pull you right off the road with it. You're better off staying here."

But where, with four animals? I immediately got on the Internet with my cell phone and looked up accommodations in Van Horn. There were very few motels and no vacancies because of all the truckers who were getting stranded as well. Only three were listed as having pet rooms. One was already full. I called one of the remaining two, and the man said he only had one room left, and all it had was a space heater, but we were welcome to use it. Now we are in freezing weather, with thin California blood and one space heater for the five of us? I decided to call the third, our last resort, and gratefully got a room booked by the time Frank came out of the men's room. He was shocked and relieved. So, we made our way the short distance in this small town to our cabin-like room and were able to park our rig nearby so that we could keep an eye on it.

Again, the dogs were ecstatic over their adventure, and the cat just quietly tolerated every noise and jolt he was put through within his crate. But now we had another problem. All of our hotel rooms across the country were off by a day. We had paid up front, and it was all non-refundable. Something else to pray about! Frank got on the phone in Van Horn after we settled in and started calling ahead. It took a long while, but he was able to explain to each vendor our weather difficulties. Each was gracious and understood the undeniable fix we were in because they, too, were experiencing the unexpected freezing rains. Each one afforded us refunds on the remaining three nights' rooms.

The next morning, we heard a sixteen-wheeler start its engine, and we knew it was time to go. Follow the truckers! They will know when and if it is safe. We loaded up as fast as we could and got to our main route to go over the pass to Odessa, a two-hour drive. It was a slight incline, and, sure enough, there were abandoned cars tipped here and there on their sides, and we were thankful we were not among them. As we drove along I-20, which would take us north from the southern route we were on, the landscape was pure ice, but the asphalt road was dry as a bone. It was beautiful to behold as the ice crystals reflected the newly risen sun shining over the distance.

Another five hours past Odessa, we hit Dallas, and, by that time, the ice storm had passed through, but we could see the effects of it all over the city. We were grateful to the Lord for protecting and directing us again, opening up a patch of blue sky above us and a dry, secure road beneath us. We were always either in front of or behind a storm but never in it. While Frank drove, I searched the Internet on my iPhone for pet rooms in Dallas and was able to secure one that would accommodate at least two pets. I had to do some fast talking to seek sympathy as to why we needed to bring in four animals. Again, since the businesses in the area were suffering the same fate from the severe ice storm, they were very understanding and accommodating, although we still got the usual stares as we piled in through the lobbies of each place we stayed. Thankfully, most people were dog lovers, and ours were so cute and friendly that they often brought smiles mingled with looks of incredulity.

After two more days with one more overnight, we arrived at our destination—a beautiful rental farmhouse deep in the country of a township called Schuyler, of "Walton's

Mountain" fame. We felt like "Hollywood" was following us or vice versa!

And, wouldn't you know, the day after we arrived, it snowed! The first snowfall was especially enjoyable, as we watched the dogs tentatively venturing out, finally romping and chasing one another, flinging the snow up in the air with their noses. They were beside themselves with excitement playing in this new, cold, white stuff they'd never seen before!

But it wasn't long before we were overwhelmed with the sparseness, loneliness, darkness, distances, deer, and huge spiders of country living. It was seventeen miles to the nearest country grocery store and the nearest vet.

After three weeks of settling in, Frank and I both started our new jobs at Jim Price Chevrolet in Charlottesville (a fifty-minute drive). One morning, I didn't feel well, so I stayed home. By God's providence, that saved Sugar's life because I was there to observe her throwing up blood. Nausea is one thing, but blood is another! I quickly took her to the vet in Livingston, where she threw up blood again. I suspected she had gotten a sliver from a small chicken bone from our dinner the night before when a piece accidentally fell to the floor and, perhaps, it was lodged within her system. But that vet didn't have a scope, so they recommended the emergency vet clinic in Charlottesville and called ahead for me. I quickly scooped Sugar up and drove the hour to get her there, by which time she was limp and laying still. I carried her inside, called Frank to come over to us from work, and, within the hour, the vet notified us that Sugar was bleeding quite profusely internally. He asked if she had gotten into any kind of poison? Not that we knew of! What did we know—we had never had to use anything of that nature in California! But when he mentioned D-Con, I remembered seeing that label around the farmhouse that was hidden in the basement or closets.

Sure enough, he said Sugar had ingested some rat poison, and we were about to lose her if a decision wasn't made quickly. Her vital organs would begin to bleed out, and she would die. The "silver lining," the vet said, was that the sliver of chicken bone that scratched her insides was causing the bleeding in her stomach before the poison had time to work on her vital organs. He could stop the bleeding by administering Vitamin K intravenously with an overnight hospital stay. It would cost us about $2300—and it took us about five seconds to decide between us that she was worth it! We were so happy to pick her up the next day, and she recuperated quickly.

That was enough country living for us, however, and we were no longer at peace about trying to rent again so, within three months, we were able to purchase a home in a more populated area with a house that actually had a fenced in backyard (not too common in farm country) on a quarter acre. The dogs enjoyed the space, and we breathed easier knowing they would not be chasing deer in the dead of night through the dense woods or being chased by bears, raccoons, or whatever else was out there threatening our peace of mind. And there would be no more rat poison or giant black spiders to tempt Sugar's palate or curiosity. Prior to our move, however, Miki was scheduled to join us in May, so I had to prepare for him fast.

CHAPTER 15

Together Again

"And now, Lord, for what do I wait?
My hope is in You."
(Psalm 39:7)

Finding a place for Miki turned out to be more of
a challenge than I had realized. In California, boarding
ranches seemed to be a dime a dozen. In Virginia, they
were plenteous because of the many popular east coast
fox-hunt clubs but were spread out all over the state, even
in the county in which we lived. Huge farms were mostly
family-owned for raising cattle or crops, which increased
the driving distances between them. The horse facilities
nearby were full, and others were either too far away or too
unkempt for what I was used to. After all, the beautiful cattle farms were money makers due to the demand for beef,
whereas many horse farms depended on individual stipends
given for lessons or boarding charges. Therefore, any prof-
its were often literally "eaten" by the horses rather than put
toward the upkeep of the facilities. I finally found a decent
but small farm about ten minutes from my new job in town,
although a thirty-mile drive from home, at least they made
a spot for him. Even though that was the same mileage
I had driven to Burbank through the years, the two-lane

country roads took longer to maneuver, and the highways were different, so it added more time to the commute wherever we went.

But it was time to send word for Miki to be sent to us, and we had him professionally hauled in a six-horse transport by a reputable company. Barbara and another dear friend, Terry, oversaw the loading process, making sure all his food and belongings were packed along with him. Jim (the friend who *loved* Virginia) had been checking in on Miki for me as well and was there to wish him Godspeed.

Miki arrived in Virginia on May 18, 2015, after a long trip across the country on the transport. It took six nights, seven days for the driver to offload other horses that were reaching their destinations during the journey and then to take on others along the way. It was an experienced outfit and the driver, Matt, kept in touch with me periodically. He said he would let me know when he reached Lynchburg, VA, which he did. I had just gotten off work and was on the highway heading home from Charlottesville to Schuyler when the call came in. That meant I only had about an hour to make the round trip–race home, hook up the horse trailer, and meet him outside Charlottesville to collect Miki and make the final transport to his new stable. Naturally, I was all thumbs trying to hook up quickly, with it getting dark and starting to rain. *Oh, help, Lord,* I cried out! I felt like an expectant mother. I hadn't seen Miki in almost four months!

Matt and I had arranged to meet off the main highway at the only place in the dark countryside that I knew would be lit up at night, being a convenience store popular for its fried chicken and gas pumps. Best of all, it had a large parking lot to accommodate his huge rig. My heart pounded with excitement as I stood on the dark corner of the little side street, watching his rig approaching with running lights lit from top to bottom. Miki was in there! Goose bumps covered my arms. It was a huge, gorgeous rig and Matt was able to spot my little truck with the two-horse trailer, lights shining in the dark, rear doors wide open awaiting its new but familiar occupant.

As Matt parked his rig and we greeted and shook hands, I started walking down the side of his long trailer, from window to window, looking for my boy. Suddenly, there he was, his white snip and lamb-shaped blaze showing through the darkness of his windowed transport stall.

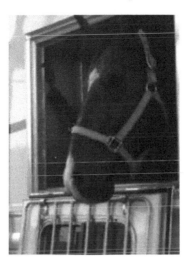

My heart leapt as tears welled up in my eyes! I sang my familiar call to him, "Miki," in a high-pitched voice which usually meant that I had a lump of sugar in my hand, and he would always come running to wherever I was standing. He remembered because, at my voice, he literally did a double-take in the window!

Matt had carefully planned the off-loading and had Miki in the last stall closest to the exit ramp. By this time, Miki was accustomed to being handled by Matt and taken on and off the transport trailer at least once a day, even to perhaps spend the night in a few horse farms across the states.

He dutifully allowed Matt to lead him down the ramp and followed him into my small trailer without hesitation. Thankfully, Miki was well acquainted with *my* trailer since we had put many miles on it together through the years— until he realized a split second later that he was being separated from his "herd" in the other trailer! Matt quickly exited the trailer stall, and we closed the back doors! Miki bugled, not wanting to be by himself. So, I hurriedly got into my truck and started moving us the rest of the way to his new farm in Charlottesville, which, again, was a forty-five-minute drive in the pitch-black countryside in the pouring rain! I held my breath then breathed out prayers along the way. By this time, it was pushing 10:00 p.m. Thankfully, my new barn manager was waiting late into the evening for our arrival, and we got Miki set up into his new stall with fresh, green, lush Virginia grass hay, which he loved, similar to the Orchard or Timothy hay that was so expensive in California. Here, it was simply the baled hay from the pastures (orchard grass). I was not surprised that the cheaper west coast alfalfa hay was, of course, more expensive on the east coast. That was not an issue now because I no longer had to pay extra for the grass hay Miki was going to enjoy on a daily basis.

Foraging the sweet grass on a hillside or in the pasture was a little bit of heaven for him, a stark pleasant change from the dry-lot stabling in which he had lived. I was advised, however, that it was necessary to slowly acclimate him to free-grazing, which had never been his custom. Beginning on day one, May 19, he was allowed to graze an hour a day for three days, then two hours a day for three days, adding another hour every three days until June 9, for a total of twenty-four days, when he was able to eat pasture grass to his heart's content for eight consecutive hours. During this time, however, it was important to monitor his output; loose, unformed stools could indicate digestive upset likely correlated to the increased sugars (fructans) being stored in the newly grown grass, preparing itself for the rest of the season. Of course, horses love the sweetness, and all horses need to be monitored more carefully in the spring. Thankfully, Miki acclimated well thanks to the careful attention of our new barn manager.

He felt right at home... despite encountering through the next few years the Virginia bugs, which were a major adjustment for both of us, having come from a virtual "no bugs m' lady" west coast climate!

Over the next three years, in an attempt to get him somewhat closer to me, I boarded Miki at two other farms where we made a few friends and enjoyed the beautiful countryside, pastures, and riding trails along flowing rivers that are the "eye candy" of central Virginia. This was especially enjoyable for both him and me since the trails in California had been basically rugged, dry, and mountainous. It was wonderful to walk on grass or pathways that were not hard-packed fire roads. Miki was a real trooper, and, with ears perked, he eyeballed every squirrel, hawk, woodpecker, vulture, and even cattle grazing on the other side of the river. But he never refused to go forward and became very relaxed with the new sights and sounds. With tutoring from a new riding buddy, Jill, I began to recognize the flora and the fauna myself, enjoying the various wildflowers growing along the way. Springtime was especially lovely, with the flowering trees and the hidden frogs or katydids making music for us as we passed by. It was a special time in our lives.

In fact, Jill and I pastured our horses together, and they became fast "buds" just like she and I did. She loved Eli as much as I loved Miki, but Eli had developed a condition that made him unrideable, so she rode an extra horse owned by the barn named Noche. He became a calm, secure trail partner for Miki, and Jill became the official tour guide as we traversed hill and dale. However, Miki was "attached at the hip" with Eli while they were in the pasture, or should I say, "attached at the withers."

The care of pastured horses on the East coast was much different than what I was accustomed to, however, but probably the way horses were meant to live. After all, space and property in California were so expensive that the boarded horses were usually in a 12 x 12 box stall and had to be turned out into a small paddock to stretch their legs or put on a hot-walker that took them in a circle for thirty minutes, or best yet, be longed or ridden often by their owners. That had been Miki's lifestyle for twenty-four years. Now he found himself out in a lush pasture for twelve hours at a time. In the spring, when he arrived, we put him out for just a few hours as I said to acclimate him to the grass slowly so he wouldn't get sick. Eventually, he stayed out until the evening feeding of various grains back in the barn where he would spend the night. However, because of the flying insects, with horse flies being the largest and worst, the horses had to stay in their stalls during the heat of the summer days and be put out at night when it was cooler and less bothersome.

The winter was the opposite—turning out during the day and staying in at night. That seemed like a good arrangement to me; however, there were many days or nights when I knew he was out that I fretted for him because of wild lightning storms, which he had never experienced in his life, or heavy rain or even snow. I bought him a special heavy winter blanket because he was accustomed to being blanketed in California when the temperature dropped below forty-five degrees, which was considered cold there. Here, the nights could go into the teens—some barn managers believed in blanketing, others didn't. Certain aspects of Miki's care were taken out of my hands which was difficult for me to monitor simply because of the distances. The various barn owners were watchful, however, and kept the horses in if the weather was too threatening at any particular time, especially if I made a special request. Miki went right along with it and seemed none the worse for wear for the first three years, as far as I could tell. But at least now he had Eli with him, and I had Jill to ask a million questions of if I ever fretted about anything. Miki and I, and Jill and Noche enjoyed our arena and trail riding at least three times a week, weather permitting, for several wonderful years.

CHAPTER 16

The Shadow of Death

"Yea, though I walk through the valley
of the shadow of death,
I will fear no evil, for You are with me."
(Psalm 23:4, NKJV)

After about four years, however, Miki finally had to
retire at a fourth farm, a Thoroughbred rehabilitation center
aptly called Rose Retreat, in an attempt to help him heal
from two bowed tendons and an old shoulder injury that
kept acting up. We couldn't figure out how he bowed his
tendons other than to assume that he was jumping around
at night in the pasture when or if the deer were hopping
over the fences. This meant absolutely no riding, but I still
traveled the distance at least three times a week as was my
custom, just to visit and pamper him with treats. The new
barn manager, Larry, who did absolutely everything and
anything the horses in his care needed, even groomed Miki
for me. His coat was always shiny, and his tail conditioned
like silk. But when I showed up, Larry said he quickly exited the stall because Miki would forget Larry was there and
concentrate on me—after all, I was the carrot, apple, cookie
Mama. Larry said laughingly that it wasn't worth his get-

ting stepped on accidentally when Miki only had eyes for me. Of course, I loved hearing that! Miki's legs began to improve under Larry's expert wrapping, icing, and eventual hand-walking. He even got to the point where he could be put out into a very small round pen so he could enjoy being in the sun and grazing on the grass again.

But at that stage in his life, he was finally beginning to show his age even though he still looked beautiful and younger than he was; however, being on total stall rest for eight or more weeks with the two bowed tendons did not do him well in the final analysis. It's not healthy for *any* horse to just stand around, especially for a geriatric equine that had always been worked in an arena or on trail; the stall rest was detrimental. A horse in pain will attempt to compensate by shifting its weight to another appendage, just as people do. Despite being on pain medication, Miki got to the point where his hind end began to weaken, and it became obvious when he walked that he was beginning to wobble. Then it became difficult for him to stand up once he laid down. The pain in his legs began aggravating his previously sore shoulder, along his spine, and to his rump, making him want to lay down more often and for longer periods of time in order to get his weight off his sore limbs.

Barbara had told me that his sire, Modern Creation, at age twenty-four, had gone down in his stall and was unable to get up at all! I did not want that to happen to Miki. It is fearful for a horse since they are prey animals and lying down is a very vulnerable position. Normally, they only lie down when they feel safe. As it was, he could get up but had to lean his hips on the side of the stall for a moment to get his feet under him and get his balance.

Six months later, on May 20 of 2019, Miki had to be put down just two days after the fourth anniversary of his arrival in Virginia and three days before his 28th birthday. We had been partners together for twenty-four wonderful years.

Miki's dedicated caregiver, Larry, was monitoring Miki's struggles and called me that fateful morning to tell me he was lying down longer and longer, and it did not look good for him. I left work immediately and started the hour's drive. I called Larry as I drove and told him I didn't know what to do, and he informed me he had already called the vet, had already asked the farm owner permission to bury Miki there if that was what I decided needed to happen, and had called the man who would dig the grave to get there as soon as he could that day. It all seemed like a dream to me, not all bad, but all sorrowful. Larry and the others there did so much for me and for him on that difficult day. I was in a daze, at a loss, and numb at the things that had to be done and that were happening right before me.

I also called my dear friend of two and a half years from our previous farm, Jill, to alert her what was about to happen. She attempted to comfort my tears and offered to come be with us. I said no. I had seen a horse go "down" before, and it is not a pleasant experience, especially because of its size dropping to the ground. I didn't want to put her through that. "Are you sure," she said, "because I'm very willing to come right now." No, I assured her. I would be okay. We hung up the phone, and it took me about ten seconds to call her back in tears and say, "Yes, please come! I do need you there!" She was the only one in Virginia who loved us both and could be moral support not only for me but also for Miki, and who would totally understand my impending trauma.

By the time I got there, Miki was out of his stall, thankfully, and in a small pipe round pen on the grass. Jill had already arrived. We fed Miki a whole bag of carrots, two apples, a couple of homemade horse muffins lovingly brought by Jill, and he even had his grain for lunch. Thankfully, he had an appetite. Larry came by to drive me up to the site where we could possibly bury Miki. We found a beautiful spot; very near Larry's recently passed racehorse, Pick-A-Fight. I was so honored to be able to share in that precious, beautifully green, and lush area for Miki's final resting place. Larry even mowed it for us! Jill had stayed with Miki for fifteen minutes while we were gone and told me that he nickered when he saw me return. I couldn't hear that from where I was approaching, but I saw his ears perk and his attention pinned on me as I walked toward them. When she told me later, it tore at my heartstrings because our affection was so mutual, especially since I didn't have any more carrots, cookies, or sugar lumps in my hand!

I struggled with the timing of things—it all seemed to happen so fast—all my hopes for Miki's rehabilitation downgraded quickly. But the Lord graciously, in several ways, confirmed to me that the timing was perfect for my Miki. We could tell he *really* was hurting despite all the medication we had him on, and to prolong that for my sake would have been cruel to him. In fact, years earlier, Jill had written "A Horse's Prayer To Us," which she had shared with me when we first met. For horse lovers like us, it is powerful and sentimental, especially this one paragraph from the equine perspective:

> Most importantly, dear friend, a true test of your love and devotion lies ahead, and I willingly entrust myself to your care. When I am old or sick or in great pain, please do not ignore my suffering or make unnecessary heroic efforts to keep me going because you do not want to let me go. Use the fierceness of your love for me to see that my life is ended lovingly, gently, and with dignity. I will know that my life was always safest in your loving heart and hands. Help me leave you and this earth knowing with my last breath that you are with me and that I will remain in your heart and memory forever, for you will remain in mine. Let my last sight on earth be your loving face, even if you are sad and crying. Let me hear the gentle sound of your voice and your touch for the last time to comfort me and to say goodbye, for I too am sad to leave you.[xiii]

Jill had taken some final pictures of us together before we transported him up the hill in Larry's trailer.

As I studied the pictures days later, I could see the pain in his eyes that were half-mast and not looking alert and happy at all. His eyes didn't reveal that to me when I was with him because the tears in my eyes clouded my own vision, but his shifting weight off his sore legs and his wobbly behind made it clear, as confirmed by Larry. Plus, he wasn't interested in eating the grass he was standing on. That was a first. I am so glad I didn't wait!

Larry took absolutely every ounce of pressure off me so that all I had to do was concern myself with Miki's welfare and comfort. He brought his stock trailer over to the round-

pen where we were and loaded Miki for me, inviting me to
be in the stall with him as we lightly bounced our way up
the pasture to where the gravesite would be. That way, Miki
wouldn't have to try to walk it. Thankfully, Jill rode with
us in the back.

The vet, Dr. Doug, was so gentle and compassionate
with Miki and me that I'm sure Miki thought he was on
another adventure with his mom and had not an ounce of
fear. When he administered the final injection as Miki stood
there, he asked us to stand back because this 1150 lb. animal was about to go down.

But Doug took Miki's halter in his hands, literally
pressing his forehead against Miki's forehead, saying
soothingly over and over again, "What a good boy, what

a good boy" while simultaneously gently pushing against him. As Miki's legs began to buckle, Doug turned his head and neck and helped him to just roll gracefully down on his side. What a gift that was to me in helping to mitigate his trauma and mine! Doug then told us to quickly come and talk to him. Jill and I raced to him, bending low to the ground at his head. I just called him like I always had, "Miki, Miki" in my sing-song way when I had a lump of sugar for him. Of course, he could hear for a few seconds before he was gone. I lovingly petted his face as I watched his eyes turn into an unseeing stare. Then we just sat there, and Jill put her arms around me as I cried aloud in my pain and loss.

But God had been so good to Miki, and to me, in all this. There was absolutely nothing I could improve on or wish were different, except it all seemed like a sad dream. I just wanted to hang on Miki's neck one more time and sob into his mane like I used to do through the years whenever something made me especially sad. I truly felt the Lord's grace, His presence walking with me through these dear friends. The reality of facing the inevitable as we went through the process made it feel like simply a shadow. I had no fear, and neither did Miki, for "He" was with us.

That afternoon in my grief, I texted my pastor, Steve Feden, at Calvary Chapel, asking for prayer. He had been a horse farrier prior to being called by God into the pastorate, so I knew he would understand my deep loss. His poignant response comforted me because he helped me to make sense of what I was feeling, which was different from having lost various pets through the years, but I couldn't figure out why. He said that a relationship between a person and their horse is similar to a marriage—it is a partnership, one of mutual respect and dependence. So, I felt like I had lost a partner, more than a pet. Of course! I felt like my right arm had been cut off. A committed horse and rider depend on each other. Miki had learned to trust me and followed my lead. He knew I would never take him into danger on purpose. And I learned to trust him that, despite his size and strength, he would be obedient with no desire to purposely get me off his back or hurt me on the ground. In fact, after a ride, whether working in an arena or just enjoying trail together, I would always hug and pet his strong, beautiful neck, give him a sweet treat, and verbally thank him for *allowing* me to climb on his back!

Within twenty-four hours, Larry had the gravesite finished and invited me back to visit. I purchased a small granite gravestone engraved with his name and dates, adding "Miki's Missionary Journey… continues." Larry eventually put mulch down on the grave so it wouldn't get muddy in the rain.

I am so thankful that Miki's final three years of life were spent in the beautiful, lush, green hills of central Virginia. He ate pasture grass to his heart's content with his buddy Elijah. Two or three times a week, Jill and I walked along a tree-lined path on our mounts by the side of a beautiful river, accompanied by the farm's own herd of mule deer that perked their big round ears and stared at us as we passed by. Miki's first encounter with them caused him to stop and stare as well, perking his pointy ears in their direction. But he quickly got used to them since the herd would graze in the field outside his and Eli's big fenced pasture in the early evenings; several of them would even jump the fence and share in their grass (as the old adage says, "The grass is greener on the other side of the fence!"). What an unexpected blessing Jill and Eli were to both of us then. She shockingly lost her beloved Eli a month after Miki was gone—she sadly wasn't able to be with him, and I wasn't able to be with her! We were both stunned. Now we became attached at the heart through our mutual grief.

Jill's favorite picture of Eli.

I have been comforted playing Danny Gokey's song, "Haven't Seen It Yet," with these words that remind me of the faithfulness of our God:

> Don't forget the things that He has done before,
> And remember He can do it all once more.
> It's like the brightest sunrise waiting on the oth-
> er side of the darkest night.
> Don't ever lose hope, hold on and believe.
> Maybe you just haven't seen it…yet;[xiv]

To this day, the booklet, *Mikwaiti*, makes its rounds to believers and unbelievers alike. I am always aware of Isaiah 55:11(NKJV):

> So shall My word be that goes forth from My mouth; It shall not return to Me void, But it shall accomplish what I please, And it shall prosper in the thing for which I sent it.

After all, this is the reason we came to Virginia in the first place. As God told the apostle Paul on the Road to Damascus when he asked, *"'What shall I do, Lord?' And the Lord said… 'Get up and go on… and there you will be told of all that has been appointed for you to do'"* (Acts 22:10).

I have also enjoyed the writings of Jonathan Cahn, a Messianic Jewish Pastor who wrote in a 2014 devotional called *Sapphires* that was dated on Miki's birthday, May 23. Naturally, I had cut it out! I find it even more significant now that our equestrian ministry has made a sharp turn with Miki's passing:

Many believers, after they…don't see all they hope to see, they start lowering their expectations. But your calling does not shrink, ever. He is waiting for you to rise to it. Rise to your calling. Don't give up the calling, give up the doubt. Believe what God's plans are for your future. Believe a few sizes bigger than you are. Believe you will become a person of victory, of righteousness, a person of the Spirit, of joy, of purity, of unstoppable love, walking in the power of the resurrection, because God will only give you a calling that is perfectly tailored a few sizes too big.[xv]

Therefore, as long as I can live and breathe…

Miki's Missionary Journey continues!

CHAPTER 17

"My Hope" Is Never Lost

"For we were saved in this hope,
but hope that is seen is not hope;
for why does one still hope for what he sees?"
(Romans 8:24, NKJV)

It's a topic of discussion and a question often asked... adults and children alike wonder, "Will my beloved pet be in heaven?" And it's a subject about which some think Scripture is unclear—or is it? Biblically, I would say the answer is no, animals do not go to heaven because they do not sin, so they do not have souls that need redeeming—but keep reading—there's hope of still seeing them again!

Almost everyone who has loved and lost a favorite animal suffers unexpected grief as if they had lost a dearly beloved family member—and, in a sense, they have, albeit not a human one. Why such strong feelings? Are these emotions God intended us to have in relation to animals?

One thing we are sure of is how precious our tears are to the Lord: *"You keep track of all my sorrows. You have collected all my tears in your bottle. You have recorded each one in your book"* (Psalm 56:8, NLT). In fact, we had this conversation years ago with a very dear friend, Dr.

Greg Harris, who was professor of Bible Exposition at our local seminary. He encouraged me with the above verse as we discussed our mutual and recent losses over our fur-friends. In a personal letter to me, he wrote that the above verse "is part of my theology on this, not so much for the pets themselves, but for those who are saved who have wept over the loss of beloved pets. In some way that only God will make right in heaven, our tears for our animals are part of God's bottle.'" These tears, he says, are "lovingly in the hands of God. God must keep them for some reason... If someone saved has never cried over a pet whom they never loved, this will not be part of their tears in God's bottle. Other tears will be there, but not those."

Emotions are something that we often find in common with many animals. Dogs, in particular, are known as "man's best friend" because they so easily relate to us, understanding our struggles in an uncanny way. If a person never owned or loved a dog, then perhaps they can't relate to that statement. However, those of us who have enjoyed their companionship have found a pet canine to express happiness, sadness, fun, and fear right along with us. How happy our dog is when we come home after even a few hours of being away. How sad it is when it knows we are leaving again. They love to have fun and play ball with us, and yet many are fearful of various things, as we are when danger is near. Even then, they might put their own lives in jeopardy for the sake of protecting ours. Dogs can be intensely faithful and loyal to their masters no matter the circumstances.

Along the line of commonality, I also found it fascinating years ago that the Institute in Basic Youth Conflicts published a book called, *Character Sketches from the Pages of Scripture*, which loosely compared God-like characteristics in the Bible with those found in nature—like the loyalty and faithfulness of dogs I just mentioned. Scripture says about God: *"If we are faithless, He remains faithful, for He cannot deny Himself"* (2 Timothy 2:13). Other animals, as well, reflect certain characteristics of their Creator: wisdom (the owl), diligence (the ant), and gentleness (the deer). There are Rattlesnakes, Songbirds, Bluebirds, and even moles who make it their practice to keep their habitat clean—as the old axiom says— "Cleanliness is next to godliness."

The emotional connection of animals with humans is why so many dogs, cats, and even other kinds of animals (I've seen goats, ponies, birds, etc.) are used for "Service." They bring comfort to the bedridden in hospitals or at home; they soothe the suffering soldier who returns home with PTSD; they lead the blind and alert the deaf. They are used in the medical community to sniff out cancer cells in patients or by the armed services or police to sniff out drugs or bombs or bodies (like at the infamous "9/11" twin towers). They even put themselves in harm's way as they loyally fight alongside their human companions. How often have we leaned on their kindness and compassion when we are

at home struggling with heartache? There's nothing sweeter than having an understanding dog on your lap licking
away the tears or an affectionate kitty to cuddle. They can
be calming to the emotional discomfort of many travelers,
even on planes!

Horses, as well, have a unique emotional connection
with their "person." There were countless times when I buried my face in Miki's big muscular neck, unloading a boat-
load of tears over one thing or another. A horse will pick up
on his rider's emotional state, whether in a good mood or
bad, and are thereby very therapeutic. Horses are often used
to help the healing process of abused children or people,
even for the handicapped. In fact, there are equine-assist-
ed therapies all over the country that can be used to treat
depression, anxiety, eating disorders, addiction, and even
those incarcerated in prisons. Therapy with horses helps
people to achieve emotional stability, growth, and learning.
Just as they can feel a fly landing on their thick hide, so
they can sense our frame of mind. In fact, a horse's "obedience" (from our perspective) is often reflective of the
personality of its person. There is much we can learn from
our equine partners. Here is an intuitive verse from a card I
received from a friend that encourages *us* to be more horse-
like, even in the service of others:

> Take life's hurdles in stride
> Loosen the reins
> Be free spirited

Keep the burrs from under your saddle
Carry your friends when they need it
Keep stable
Gallop to greatness!^{xvi}

When we can relate with our own animals through our emotions, no wonder we feel such emptiness when they are taken by death or loss. A poignant insight was made by the 1973 Pulitzer Prize winner, Konrad Lorentz, who said:

> The fidelity of a dog is a precious gift demanding no less moral responsibility than the friendship of a human being. The bond with a dog is as lasting as the ties of this earth can ever be.

I, of course, could easily apply that to the friendship or partnership of a horse.

"Men and women are similar to animals in having flesh, soul, and spirit, but the critical difference is that we are made in the image of God," says Dr. David Eckman from Becoming What God Intended Ministries.^{xvii} Even though "man" was made in the image of God, Adam marred that image through his choice to sin by disobeying and turning his back on his Creator. On the contrary, the animals that were instilled with the character qualities of their Creator still reflect some of those characteristics despite the fact that they are now under the curse of sin caused by man! There are those who would want to credit animal reactions only and purely to instinct which, by the way, is real and is infused into them by a Creator God who looks out for their welfare and ours:

> *Even the stork in the sky knows her seasons; and the turtledove and the swift and the thrush observe the time of their migration. But my people do not know the ordinance of the Lord* (Jeremiah 8:7).

And:

> *But now ask the beasts, and let them teach you; And the birds of the heavens, and let them tell you. Or speak to the earth, and let it teach you; And let the fish of the sea declare to you. Who among all these does not know That the hand of the* LORD *has done this, In whose hand is the life of every living thing, And the breath of all mankind* (Job 12:7-10).

In other words, God cares about all of His creatures: *"You,* LORD, *preserve both people and animals"* (Psalm 36:6, NIV), and so do we care about those we've been privileged to know: *"A righteous man has regard for the life of his animal"* (Proverbs 12:10). Animals glorify God by acting like what they are because they did not sin in the Garden. Adam did, and we, as Adam's progeny, have spiritually inherited the same disobedient nature of sin! Obviously, animals do not sin since they do exactly as God has created them; however, they are physically, mentally, and emotionally affected by the sin of Adam that brought a curse on *all* of creation. Therefore, as I said, it is my contention that animals do not need to go to heaven since they do not *need* to be redeemed from their own sin. They not only obey their Creator completely and do not sin, but they even praise Him by being who and what they are: *"Praise the Lord from the earth, sea monsters and all deeps; ...Beasts and all cattle"* (Psalm 148:7,10). So, they do not need to be "saved" from eternal hell and rescued into the spiritual, eternal life of heaven as mankind does. But there's more!

Only when we humans turn to our Creator God and believe that forgiveness has been provided because of what Jesus Christ did on the cross by dying in our place—only then do we glorify God as our fellow creatures, the animals, do. The promise to us is to have peace with God in this life and everlasting life with Him in the future. After all, He has set a sense of eternity into the heart of man (Ecclesiastes 3:11). The promise to animals, however, is the eventual reversal of the curse they've been under since Adam's sin in the Garden. That is revealed in Romans 8:18-23:

> *For I consider that the sufferings of this present time are not worthy to be compared with the glory that is to be revealed to us. For the anxious longing of the creation waits eagerly for the revealing of the sons of God. For the creation was subjected to futility, not willingly, but because of Him who subjected it, in hope that <u>the creation itself also will be set free from its slavery to corruption</u> into the freedom of the glory of the children of God. For*

*we know that <u>the whole creation groans and suf-
fers the pains of childbirth together until now.</u> And
not only this, but also we ourselves, having the first
fruits of the Spirit, even we ourselves groan within ourselves, waiting eagerly for our adoption as
sons, the redemption of our body.*

The creation is more than just flowers and trees. In
fact, the animals eat those! That being said, animals, being
a major part of creation, "wait eagerly" for the time when
this cursed earth is finally replaced with the New Earth
as promised in Revelation 21. There we will inhabit the
glorious, physical, eternal, new Paradise-found with our
immortal bodies. So, too, it is my contention that animals
will inhabit the New Earth as it was always meant to be for
them. There will be no more suffering for them either, and
their immortal bodies will be just as glorious as will ours
because they will be as God originally intended, without
the curse caused by *man's* sin. After all, their spirit comes
from the breath of God (Ecclesiastes 3:18-21). I can only
imagine how beautiful they will be with the curse on creation lifted!

A biblically astute and scholarly book I've read, *Cold
Noses at the Pearly Gates* by Gary Kurz, gives some further encouraging insights:

> It is not a stretch of either truth or imagination to
> assume that all animals originally existed in a "pet"
> status *(with Adam)*. It is convincingly apparent that

this was precisely the role God had intended for them.[xviii]

With that thought in mind and carefully reading through the Genesis account, it is safe to draw the conclusion that, from the very beginning, God had a perfect plan and a purpose for Adam's relationship with the animals so that he personally named each one at God's instruction. Their environment was perfect from the start; there was no fear between them prior to Adam's fall, so each approached the other in total compatibility and companionship. Being herbivores, no animal was afraid of being eaten by another or by Adam! We can just picture Adam petting the heads or scratching the chins of each kind, dubbing them with their appropriate nomenclature—and they, in turn, receiving his touch and tone with much tranquility. The only thing missing was a companion fit for Adam himself—thus, God created Eve. All of that being accomplished, *"God saw all that He had made, and behold, it was very good"* (Genesis 1:31).

Another excellent book that totally comforted me in this regard years ago when I lost some of my beloved pets was Heaven, by Randy Alcorn. Pastor Alcorn expounds in Chapter 13 of his book on these biblical truths with these reasonable thoughts:

> Because animals were a significant part of life on the original earth and Scripture makes it clear that God will remake the earth just as He will remake mankind, it stands to reason that animals will be

part of the New Earth (Why wouldn't they be?).

We're told that animals, along with all creation, long for the deliverance that will be theirs at the time of the redemption of our bodies, at the resurrection (Romans 8:19, 23). They await and long for it, because they will be part of it.

As the entire creation, including animals, plants, and nature itself, fell on humanity's coattails, so shall the entire creation rise on our coattails, as beneficiaries of Christ's redemptive work.

He goes on to say:

Since according to Romans 8 it is those presently suffering and groaning who will be delivered, it's likely that some *(if not all)* of the same animals on the present Earth will be remade to live on the New Earth. *(Italics mine)*.[xix]

I am, therefore, drawing these conclusions: since there was no fear of man by the animals God created in the Garden before Adam's sin, and since all the animals we would label today as wild had a perfect relationship with Adam, God compassionately understands our emotional connection with our own animals that we have been privileged to tame and call pets. They have been caught up in the curse of our sin, ours alone and not theirs. Therefore, it excites me to think that someday, in the eternal state or New Earth, I too can pat the head of a funny armadillo or rub the long neck of a giraffe, like Adam did, or once again be reunited with the pets I have loved and that have been attached to me.

Also, Scripture plainly speaks of horses being ridden by Christ and His armies when He returns to conquer evil, to demolish the curse of sin in the present earth. We also read of wolves, lambs, lions, calves, and snakes living in harmony again in the 1,000-year millennial kingdom established at Christ's return. Therefore, might not our horses, dogs, and cats, etc., which we have personally known, be included or re-created, not in the millennium, but in the final New Earth? Just as we will know one another, we will know them! After all, the disciples knew Jesus after His death when He rose from the dead in His immortal, glorified body:

> When therefore it was evening, on that day, the first day of the week, and when the doors were shut where the disciples were, for fear of the Jews, Jesus came and stood in their midst, and said to them, "Peace be with you." And when he had said this, he showed them both his hands and his side. The disciples therefore rejoiced when they saw the Lord (John 20:19, 20).

> "We know that when He appears, we will be like Him, because we will see Him just as He is" (1 John 3:2).

This kind of study offers much food for thought and, for

me, brought much comfort after the loss of Mikwaiti ("My Hope"), especially since he was my partner in ministry for twenty-four years. I do hope, dear reader, that it brings a sense of joy and comfort to your heart as we stop and contemplate the wonderful "hope" that has been gifted to us, remembering that whatever God does in this regard in the future is good—because He does all things well (Mark 7:37)! This is touched on in the Theological Wordbook of the Old Testament:

> Hope has an eternal home in man's heart. As long as there is a future, there is hope (Prov.23:18; probably an eternal future is intended). But only the believer can really express his hope in the future, for it belongs to Yahweh alone. Zechariah calls God's people, *"prisoners of hope."* And he summons them to look forward to experiencing God's restoration (Zech.9:12).[xx]

Ecclesiastes 3:19 says,

> *The fate of the sons of men and the fate of beasts is the same. As one dies so dies the other; indeed, they all have the same breath and there is no advantage for man over beast.*

Keeping in mind, however, that the promise of restoration is not only to those who love God but also to that which He loves in His magnificent creation. Therefore, we eagerly look forward to the New Heaven and the New

Earth and all that encompasses. It is as though the Lord were saying to me personally about Miki, "His breath of life came from me and has returned to me; you will see him again."

An Internet article by Christian Anthropologist, Daniel Hoffman, says:

> Genesis 2 describes God breathing into man the "breath of life," but that language is not unique to man, as it is also used of animal life a bit later in the flood story (Genesis 7:22). So there is no "soul vs. non-soul" distinction at creation, nor am I aware of any other biblical texts that make such a distinction. Ecclesiastes 3:19 actually speaks of men and beasts all having "one spirit" (רֽוּחַ אֶחָד, translated in the ESV as "the same breath;" cf. Psalm 104:29-30). ...As far as biblical language is concerned, creaturely life is simply creaturely life, whether human or animal. ...to assert that humans are "body and soul" and animals are only "body" has no basis in the text of Scripture that I can see, and no relation to man's position as image of God.[xxi]

A dear friend, among many, sent me a stirring sympathy card at Miki's passing which was in itself stunning because the cover looked so much like him—a pinto with four white socks. It said on the inside, "Not gone, just waiting patiently at the end of the trail." My enthusiastic response to that thought is: "Someday, by God's perfect will and sweetness of grace, He will turn my bottle of tears for Miki into tears of joy when I meet him on that heavenly trail."

Lest you think these thoughts are coming from an emotionally attached, sentimental person, consider this: the Lord Jesus and I will ride horses into the millennial kingdom together! After all, Revelation 19:14 says: *"And the armies of heaven, (those of us who have gone before) arrayed in fine linen, white and pure, were following him on white horses."*

What about you? Will you also be riding alongside Jesus Christ, the coming victorious Messiah, when He returns? So why not ride on the New Earth together as well? Perhaps Miki's spots will stand out among the herd of white horses!

Mr. Hoffman's conclusion is as mine:

> Is it at all conceivable that our eternal state in the new creation (pictured in Revelation 21-22) would not contain as rich or richer an assortment of animal life as God made at creation in the beginning?[xxii]

As my friend, Greg Harris, encouragingly concluded: "Who knows what our heavenly Father has in store for us in our ultimate home. I could easily see it shared with this aspect of God's creation. After all, animals were a part of God's creation He originally called good, and *'Every good thing bestowed and every perfect gift is from above, coming down from the Father of lights, with whom there is not variation or shifting shadow'* (James 1:17). ...So, stay tuned, ...and don't be surprised if God does not inhabit your heavenly dwelling place, which He prepares with each one of His children in mind, with things uniquely made for each one of us."

My final conclusion then, simply stated for your consideration, is this: from among all of the animals and creation that Christ has redeemed according to Romans 8:18-23 above, He will present our specific animals back to us in the eternal state of the New Earth. They will not be strangers but will be the pets that we have known and loved. That is part of our reward, and what an awesome reward it will be!

Epilogue

God knows us so intimately and is involved in our lives in such a personal way that He custom-makes a tender mercy for every specific trial we might face. Our God is a God of such great love that it is infinitely beyond imagining—and that love is directed toward us. After all, He gave His beloved Son, Jesus, who died—even voluntarily laid down His life for us—to prove that love (John 3:16). Why, oh, why do we fret as though no One cares? Whatever problem, difficulty, or heartache we face, God wants to communicate Himself and His love to us *in* the affliction. There is no problem, no matter how great, that can separate us from His love.

> *For I am convinced that neither death, nor life, nor angels, nor principalities, nor things present, nor things to come, nor powers, nor height, nor depth, nor any other created thing, will be able to separate us from the love of God, which is in Christ Jesus our Lord* (Romans 8:38-39).

Have you ever been afraid in the physical sense of being seriously injured? Or have there been times in life when you feared other less tangible things? We can call on God in those times of fear as well. He is the God of the past, present, and future as explained in Hebrews 13:8, *"Jesus Christ is the same yesterday and today, yes and forever."*

He knows the end from the beginning and calls Himself *"the Alpha and the Omega"* (the First and the Last) in Revelation 21:6. He alone is totally reliable and trustworthy according to 2 Samuel 22:31b-32, which says, *"The word of the Lord is tested; He is a shield to all who take refuge in Him. For who is God, besides the Lord? And who is a rock, besides our God?"* Being saved from dangerous situations like I was with Fahrenheit, Liponio, and even Miki, illustrated the faithfulness and power of my God to rescue me from any danger, seen or unseen, real or imagined. All I have to do is trust Him, to *"fear no evil, for Thou art with me"* (Psalm 23:4, KJV).

But He doesn't promise protection at all times because even injury and death are used according to His perfect will and plan for each of us, but He is able! The Bible narrative in the Old Testament about the three famous Jewish captives in Babylon named Shadrach, Meshach, and Abednego, relates that they knew God's love and power well and told King Nebuchadnezzar of their trust, whether God would save them—or not. They were threatened with a fiery death for not worshipping a false idol:

> *If it be so, our God whom we serve is able to deliver us from the furnace of blazing fire; and He will deliver us out of your hand, O king. But if not, let it be known to you, O king, that we are not going to serve your gods or worship the golden image that you have set up (Daniel 3:17-18).*

An Eternal Hope

Ever since I became a Christ-follower in 1972, God has shown His loving-kindness to me again and again, and my equestrian career is but one illustration of that. *My hope* is that those who read these stories will know His loving-kindness as well, for He promises to manifest it to all who trust Him.

What does it mean to trust God? It means believing in Jesus, the Son of God, as one's Savior and Lord. Why is that necessary? Because the Bible says, *"...all have sinned and fall short of the glory of God"* (Romans 3:23). Each of us is a sinner. All of us fail to meet God's perfect standards because anything we say, think, or do that is less than perfect is sin. Because of our sin, we cannot enter heaven, the sinless dwelling place of God the Father.

The Bible also says that *"...the wages of sin is death"* (Romans 6:23a). The wage or payment we receive for our sins is the penalty of death—not just physical death, which is the separation of our spirit from our body, but also spiritual death, which means our spirit would be separated forever from heaven and God Himself. Just as we have been born in the flesh, Jesus said we must also be born in the Spirit, i.e., born again: "That which is born of the flesh is flesh, and that which is born of the Spirit is spirit. Do not be amazed that I said to you, 'You must be born again'" (John 3:6-7). Thus, God made provision to avoid the second spiritual death: "For God so loved the world, that He gave His only begotten Son, that whoever believes in Him shall not perish, but have eternal life" (John 3:16).

The Good News, however, is that *"...the free gift of God is eternal life in Christ Jesus our Lord"* (Romans 6:23b). Jesus died on the cross to pay sin's penalty so that all who trust in Him as Savior and Lord will not die spiritually but live forever with Him in heaven. The Bible says, *"...as many as received Him, to them He gave the right to become children of God, even to those who believe in His name..."* (John 1:12).

What should a sinner's response be toward Jesus Christ? The Bible says, *"...if you confess with your mouth Jesus as Lord, and believe in your heart that God raised Him from the dead, you will be saved"* (Romans 10:9-10). Verse 13 says that if you *"call upon the name of the Lord, [you] will be saved."* Calling upon the Lord involves both repentance (turning from willful sin) and faith (believing God and His Word). The Lord desires that we call upon Him, for the Bible also says: *"Call to Me and I will answer you and tell you great and unsearchable things you do not know"* (Jeremiah 33:3), and:

> *Therefore, the Lord longs to be gracious to you, and therefore He waits on high to have compassion on you. For the Lord is a God of justice; how blessed are all those who long for Him* (Isaiah 30:18).

In the midst of difficult circumstances, God showed His love to me through a horse named Mikwaiti, but that is nothing compared to the love that God showed toward me when He sent His Son to die on the cross on my behalf. By trusting in Christ and His provision on the cross, you too can be saved from sin's penalty and enjoy eternal life.

Are you willing to trust Him? If so, you may want to pray a prayer something like this: Lord Jesus, I know that I am a sinner. I ask you to forgive me of my sins, be the Lord of my life and the Savior of my soul. Please come into my heart, give me the gift of your Holy Spirit here on earth and allow me to come into your heaven, eternally with You. Thank You, Jesus. Amen.

My hope is that you will make the above prayer your own and learn to wait as the Lord works wonders in your heart through life's twists and turns.

> *I wait for the Lord, my soul does wait, and in His word do I hope. My soul waits for the Lord more than the watchmen for the morning; ...hope in the Lord; for with the Lord there is loving-kindness, and with Him is abundant redemption* (Psalm 130:5-7).

THE END

* * * * *

Note: Please enjoy a Vimeo in full color and put to music, prepared as a tribute to this wonderful horse, this wonderful gift from God!

https://vimeo.com/mikismom

(I owe a special thanks to a very talented friend,

Bill Chadwick

for his masterful editorial compilation

of our memorable moments).

* * * * *

The Best is Yet to Come
*"And the Lord blessed the latter days of Job more
than his beginning"* (Job 42:12).

Endnotes

i "Be Still My Soul," written by Katharina von Schlegel (born 1697) and melody by Jean Sibelius.

ii California Dressage Society, February 2002, V. 9, 1.2, "Meet the Juniors," by Danielle Casalett, 10.

iii Spectator's Guide to Dressage, California Dreaming Winter Dressage Circuit, "The Competitors," Los Angeles Dressage Committee, Glenda McElroy.

iv California Dressage Society, February 2002, V.9,1.2, "Meet the Juniors," by Kelsey Bullock, 9, 10.

v Spectator's Guide to Dressage, California Dreaming Winter Dressage Circuit, "The Competition" Los Angeles Dressage Committee, Glenda McElroy.

vi Ibid

vii USDF Connection, Yearbook 2000, "The Gift of Dance," by Brooke Lemke, First Place—Fiction Essay, 15-21 years old, 9.

viii Spectator's Guide to Dressage, California Dreaming Winter Dressage Circuit, "The Judging," "The Test," Los Angeles Dressage Committee, Glenda McElroy.

ix *Dressage Today,* 1999, "Reiner Klimke and Linda Tellington Jones" "Working Magic with Dressage Horses" excerpts taken by Beth Baumert, January 12, 2010 x *A Festival of Dressage* by Jane Kidd; Arco Publishing, Inc., NY, 29.

xi *Morning and Evening*, by Charles H. Spurgeon, Hendrickson Publishers, 1991, 74.

xii "Overwhelmed," written by Mike Weaver / Big Daddy Weave band

xiii "A Horse's Prayer To Us" by Jill Powell.

xiv "Haven't Seen It Yet," written By Colby Wedgeworth, Ethan Hulse & Danny Gokey

xv *Sapphires,* "The Gap & The Glory" by Jonathan Cahn, May 23, 2014

xvi "Advice From A Horse," by Leaning Tree.

xvii *Head to Heart, Experiencing God's Affectionate Acceptance*, Section Fourteen, by David Eckman, Ph.D., 133.

xviii *Cold Noses at the Pearly Gates* by Gary Kurz, pp?

xix *Heaven* by Randy Alcorn, Ch. 13.

xx R. Laird Harris, Robert Laird Harris, Gleason Leonard Archer and Bruce K. Waltke, *Theological Wordbook of the Old Testament,* electronic ed. (Chicago: Moody Press, 1999), 791.

xxi *Knowing Scripture,* "What Does the Bible Teach About Animals?" by Daniel Hoffman, Anthropology,

March 13,   2018.

   xxii   Ibid.

Note: All photographs and published quotes used by permission where needed.

CPSIA information can be obtained
at www.ICGtesting.com
Printed in the USA
JSHW051532041221
20939JS00005B/12

9 781637 696101